BALLET

Annabel Thomas
Edited by Helen Davies
Designed by Chris Scollen

Contents

2 What is ballet?
4 Getting started
6 Ballet techniques
8 Going to a class
10 Creating a ballet
12 Writing steps down
14 The structure of a ballet company
16 Putting on a ballet
18 Costumes and make-up
20 Watching a ballet
22 Ballet as a career
24 Life at a ballet school

26 Exercises at the *barre*
30 Centre work
34 Jumps and travelling steps
36 A simple dance
38 Steps for two
39 Dancing *en pointe*
40 Famous choreographers
42 Stories of ballets
44 Famous dancers
46 Ballet words
48 Index

Ballet consultant: Kate Castle

Illustrated by Ann Savage,
Peter Mennim, Chris Lyon, Kathy Wyatt
and Cathy Wood.

What is ballet?

Ballet is a way of telling a story using music and dance instead of words. It consists of patterns of movement which have developed over the centuries. The word classical describes its style. This book is all about classical ballet. Some of the influences which have helped to make up classical ballet are shown on the right.

Dancers who perform ballet on stage are highly trained. Many people learn the techniques of ballet for fun, though. It helps them to feel graceful, co-ordinated and fit.

Classical ballet is found all around the world, for instance in Europe, the USA, China, Japan and South America.

19th century ballroom dancing.

Classical ballet.

Elizabethan dancing.

Classical ballet

Early classical ballets such as *Giselle* and *La Sylphide* were created during the Romantic Movement in the first half of the 19th century. This movement influenced art, music and ballet. It was concerned with the supernatural world of spirits and magic. It often showed women as passive and fragile. These themes are reflected in the ballets of the time, called Romantic ballets.

Ballets created during the latter half of the 19th century, such as *Swan Lake*, *The Nutcracker* and *The Sleeping Beauty* represent classical ballet in the grandest form.* Their main aim was to display the techniques of classical ballet to the full.

In these ballets, complicated sequences which show off demanding steps, leaps and turns are fitted into the story.

Ballets created during this century are called Modern ballets. They do not always have a definite story line. They have a theme, though, and concentrate more on emotions and atmospheres and attempt to arouse feelings in the audience. Different people might react to them in different ways.

Romantic, Classical and Modern ballets all follow the techniques of classical ballet.

2   *This book calls ballets of this period Classical ballets, with a capital C.

Court dancing of the 15th and 16th centuries.

Folk dancing.

How ballet began

Beauchamps

The roots of classical ballet go back 500 years. It began in the courts of Italian noblemen and soon spread to the French courts. Performers danced, sang and recited poetry to entertain guests at celebrations.

The first real ballet, where mime, music and dance were combined in one performance, was called *The Comic Ballet of the Queen*. It was staged in 1581 at the French court.

Court dancer.

Louis XIV of France founded the first ballet school, called the Royal Academy of Dancing, in 1661. A ballet master at the Academy, called Beauchamps, established five positions of the feet. These are still the basis of all ballet steps.*

Other steps came from Elizabethan and folk dances. The more acrobatic steps developed from the antics of street players and circus performers and from the Italian theatre, called *La Commedia del Arte*.

When ballets were first performed, men played the female parts, disguising themselves in wigs and masks. Women were allowed to dance in public after 1681. However, they had to wear lots of bulky clothes which hampered movement.

The possibility for spectacular footwork emerged when Marie Camargo daringly shortened her dress above her ankles in the 1720s.

Shorter dress revealing ankles.

About this book

This book is both about doing ballet yourself and enjoying ballet as a member of the audience. Here are some of the things that you can find out about in the book.

You can find out what happens at a ballet class and there are step-by-step instructions for how to do some basic ballet steps.

At the end of the book, lots of ballet words are explained.

The book explains what goes on behind the scenes when a major ballet is staged. You can also find out all about wigs, costumes and how stage make-up is applied to create different characters.

The work of a choreographer, who combines dance, music and mime to create a ballet, is described. You can find out about recording ballets by writing them down, called dance notation.

There are suggestions for what to look out for when you watch a ballet and tips on where to sit in a theatre. You can find the stories of some of the most famous ballets towards the end of the book.

*You can find out what these five positions are on page 6.

Getting started

You can start ballet classes at any age, though the younger you are, the more easily your body adapts to the physical demands that ballet makes. Children of three years old can go to simple dance classes. Proper ballet lessons begin at the age of seven.

Classes are held at dancing schools, community centres and some sports centres. It is important to find a qualified teacher who will teach you the correct technique. He or she will have letters after his or her name, such as AISTD.*

What to wear

In a ballet class, you wear layers of clothing. These keep you warm when you start and you can strip them off as you get hotter. The clothes are close-fitting so the lines and shapes your body makes can easily be seen by the teacher.

Girls usually wear a leotard and pink tights which allow for plenty of freedom of movement. At the beginning of a class you may like to wear legwarmers and a crossover. This is a type of cardigan that crosses over at the front and ties at the back.

Boys wear black tights with white socks over the top and a white T shirt. You can wear a track suit until you have warmed up.

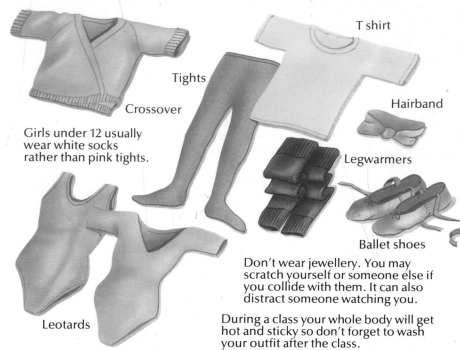

Crossover

Girls under 12 usually wear white socks rather than pink tights.

Tights

T shirt

Hairband

Legwarmers

Ballet shoes

Leotards

Don't wear jewellery. You may scratch yourself or someone else if you collide with them. It can also distract someone watching you.

During a class your whole body will get hot and sticky so don't forget to wash your outfit after the class.

How to wear your hair

Your hair needs to be off your face so it does not get in the way or make your neck hot. Most girls with long hair put it up in a bun held in a hair net, with a hairband to stop wisps flying out. You could also plait it round your head. If you have short hair you can wear a hairband to stop it falling forwards. Boys can wear sweatbands in class for the same reason.

These styles allow your whole face to be seen and give you a long neck line.

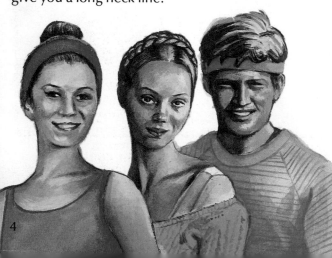

Buying your outfit

You do not need to buy any special clothing until you have been to a ballet class and know that you like it and want to carry on. Most teachers will not mind if you start in bare feet, wearing a track suit or swimming costume.

Ask your teacher where is the best place to buy your equipment. Most big department stores sell leotards, tights and track suits. You can get ballet shoes from most shoe shops.

*Associate of the Imperial Society of Teachers of Dancing.

Ballet shoes

Boys wear shoes made of soft leather, held on by elastic. Girls' shoes are made of leather or satin, kept on by elastic or ribbons tied round the ankle. You can find out how to sew on ribbons and elastic below.

A girl does not need block toed ballet shoes, called *pointe* shoes, until her teacher considers her feet and legs strong enough to dance on her toes (*en pointe*).

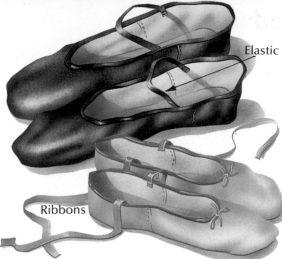

Elastic

Ribbons

Looking after your shoes

Ballet shoes are hand-made and expensive, so take care of them. Only use them for classes.

You can clean the ribbons by scrubbing them with a nail brush, soap and water. Do not get the shoes themselves wet.

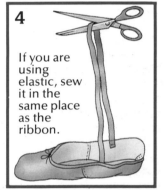

Sewing on ribbons

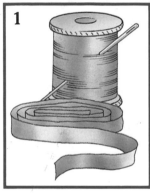

1 For each shoe, you need a strong ribbon with a non-slippery back, about 1cm (½in) wide and 1m (1yd) long.

2 To find out where the ribbon should be sewn, fold the heel forward along the sole, as shown.

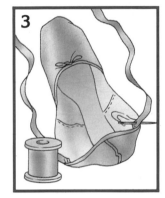

3 Position the ends of the ribbon on the inside of the shoe, either side of the fold. Then sew them firmly into place.

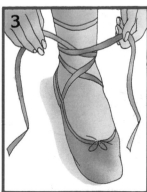

4 If you are using elastic, sew it in the same place as the ribbon.

Finally, stretch out the loop of ribbon and cut it in the middle to make two ribbons of the same length.

Tying the ribbon

When you tie the ribbons of your shoes, your foot should be flat on the floor.

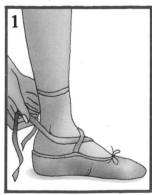

1 Bring both ribbons forward, cross them over and take them behind your ankle.

2 Cross the ribbons over behind your ankle. Then bring them round to the front again.

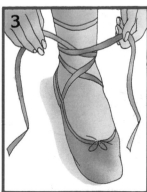

3 Cross the ribbons over once again at the front, a little above the first crossing.

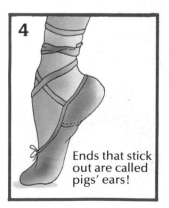

4 Finally, knot the ribbons twice at the back and neatly tuck in the loose ends.

Ends that stick out are called pigs' ears!

Ballet techniques

These two pages tell you some facts about ballet which you need to know before learning any steps. You can find out about the five positions of the feet and the seven movements of dance, which are the basis of all ballet steps.

All ballet steps have French names. This is because many steps were first introduced at the Academy of Dancing founded by King Louis XIV of France. In this book, the French names of the steps are in italics.

The five positions of the feet

Nearly every step in ballet begins and ends with one of five positions of the feet. They were devised by King Louis XIV's ballet master, Beauchamps. He worked them out so that a person's weight would be evenly placed no matter what position their body was in.

To start with, you will only use the first, second and third positions. Later, you will learn fourth and fifth and use third less. There are two fourth positions, one open and one crossed. To begin with you will probably mostly use open fourth.

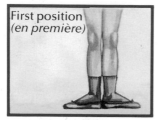
First position (*en première*)

Place your heels together and turn your feet and legs out to the sides.

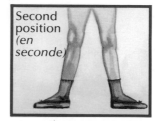
Second position (*en seconde*)

Place your feet apart by about one and a half times your foot's length. Turn them out.

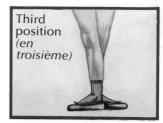
Third position (*en troisième*)

Put the heel of one foot against the middle of the other foot. Turn both feet out.

Open fourth (*en quatrième: ouverte*)

Place one foot directly forward from first position by about ⅓m (1ft).

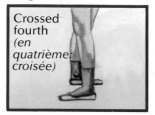
Crossed fourth (*en quatrième: croisée*)

In crossed fourth, one foot goes directly forward from fifth (see next picture).

Fifth position (*en cinquième*)

Turn both feet out, with the heel of one foot against the toes of your other foot.

Turn-out

In ballet, the feet and legs have to be turned out from the hips so that your toes and knees face sideways instead of forwards. This is called turn-out. It takes years of practice to do it properly.

Dancers first began to turn out their legs in Louis XIV's day. It showed off the calves and elegant, heeled shoes of the male dancers. Turn-out is now essential to the technique of classical ballet.

Turning your legs out enables you to lift them higher. Without it your hip joints would lock up at a certain height and the streamlined look of ballet would be impossible to achieve.

The seven movements of dance

Every step in ballet is based on one of seven dance movements. These are movements which your body can make naturally. Their French names are shown below with their English translation opposite.

Plier — to bend
Glisser — to glide
Tourner — to turn
Etendre — to stretch
Sauter — to jump
Relever — to rise
Elancer — to dart

These words are not always used in the form shown. For instance, *tendu* or *tendue* means stretched.

You can check the meaning of French words in the list of ballet words on pages 46-47.

Gliding

Darting

Bending

Turning

Stretching

Rising

Jumping

Using the seven movements

Here are some examples of ballet steps and the different movements that they use. You can find out how to do some of these steps yourself on pages 30-35.

Arabesque penché

Pas de chat

Glissade

Pirouette

This is called an *arabesque penché*. It combines stretching and raising.

This step is called a *pas de chat* (step of a cat). You dart and jump like a pouncing cat.

A *glissade* is a step where your foot glides along the ground with your knees bent.

A *pirouette* is a turning step. You turn on one leg, bend the other leg and lift it.

Classical ballet techniques

Within classical ballet there are different techniques, such as the Royal Academy of Dancing (R.A.D.), the British Ballet Organisation (B.B.O.) and the Cecchetti Society techniques. You can be examined in these techniques. There is also the Imperial Society Classical Ballet exam syllabus.

The basic movements are the same in all techniques but the combinations of steps vary and some of the arm positions differ slightly.

Going to a class

When you begin to learn ballet you should attend one or two classes a week. Regular attendance will gradually improve your technique. Professional dancers have to go to at least a class a day, as well as rehearsals, to keep in top condition and constantly to improve their ballet skills.

The picture below shows the inside of a ballet studio. At the bottom of the page you can find what to expect when you go to a class. Opposite you can see the different kinds of steps you will learn.

A wooden hand rail, called a *barre*, runs round the wall at waist level. You hold on to it for certain exercises (see next page).

Some studios have two *barres*, one higher than the other, for people of different heights.

There are full length mirrors on the wall so you can watch yourself when you dance and correct any mistakes.

This is a box of rosin. Rosin is a yellow crystal made from the sap of fir trees. If you rub the soles of your shoes in it, it breaks up into a white powder which sticks to them and stops you slipping.

There is usually a dressing room where you can leave your outdoor clothes and get changed before and after class.

A pianist usually accompanies the classes. This helps the students perform the exercises at the right pace and develops their sense of rhythm.

If there is no piano your teacher will probably use a tape recorder. Most teachers prefer a pianist, though, as he or she can adjust the speed of the music to the exercises and stop and start without delays.

A proper ballet studio has a floor with a wooden or vinyl surface. The floor is sprung which means that it "gives" very slightly beneath your feet when you jump.

What happens at a class?

All classes, no matter how advanced, follow roughly the same structure. They start with exercises at the *barre*, followed by "centre practice" (see next page) and end with jumps, turns and travelling steps.

At first you will be put in a beginners' class. Your teacher will stand where everyone can see him or her. The teacher will show how each step is done and then go around the class correcting students' movements.

Warming up at the *barre*

A class begins with gentle exercises to "warm up" your muscles, stretching them and preparing them for more demanding movements. This reduces the risk of you hurting yourself.

You warm up at the *barre,* beginning with *pliés* (knee bends). You can find out how to do *pliés* on pages 26-27.

Further exercises use your feet, ankles, knees and whole leg in more strenuous movements.

The *barre* acts as a support so you can concentrate on the alignment of one part of your body with another in harmony and balance. This is called placing.

To help your placing, imagine a line running straight down through the centre of your body, ending between your feet. Then imagine another line going straight across your hips, so both hips are level with each other.

Centre practice

You move into the middle of the room for centre practice. Here you learn how to hold your arms, called *port de bras*.

You also repeat some of the foot and leg exercises done at the *barre*, to develop strength and muscles without its support.

You then progress to more sustained movements, where, for example, you slowly raise your leg. (See pages 30-31.)

Jumps, turns and travelling steps

The latter part of the class consists of *petit allegro* and then *grand allegro*. *Allegro** is Italian for quick. *Petit* and *grand* are French for small and big.

Petit allegro consists of small jumping and turning steps. *Grand allegro* is large jumping and travelling steps. There is more about these on pages 32-35.

How to stand

Learning to stand correctly can take a lot of practice. Your head should be held up with your chin level. Relax your shoulders to lengthen your neck.

Chin level (not sticking out).

Long neck

Shoulders down

Open chest

Stomach in

Bottom in

Your stomach and bottom should be well tucked in. Carry your weight on the balls of your feet so that your heels touch the floor but do not dig in.

*Allegro is a musical term. These are always written in Italian.

Creating a ballet

The art of creating a ballet is called choreography. Someone who does this is called a choreographer. As well as new ballets, a choreographer may develop a new version of an old ballet.

Most ballet companies employ a choreographer. New ballets keep the dancers in the company enthusiastic and keep audiences interested in the company.

A ballet may tell a story or create a particular atmosphere. Nowadays, though, some ballets are devoted to movement for its own sake.

The idea for a new ballet may be sparked off by a poem, piece of music, story, play, painting, or even a single dancer's talent.

The dancer Lynn Seymour inspired the choreographer Kenneth MacMillan to create works for her. The American contemporary dance choreographer, Twyla Tharp, created works for the classical dancer, Mikhail Barishnikov.

How choreographers work

Choreographers are usually trained dancers with first-hand knowledge of the steps they use. They begin by getting to know the music for a new ballet before starting work with the dancers.

Most choreographers first work out what effects they want to achieve, with a framework of steps. Then they work on the steps with the dancers to find the best movements.

Choreographers seldom work straight through a ballet. They usually begin with parts for one or two dancers. Then they develop the small group dances and leave the big groups until last.

Most companies have resident ballet teachers. They watch the choreographer at work so that they get to know the steps of a new ballet. This means they can rehearse the dancers later.

As a ballet is choreographed, the steps are recorded in a kind of shorthand called notation so that they are not forgotten. You can find out more about ballet notation on pages 12-13.

Costume and scenery must be in keeping with the style of a ballet and the choreographer's intentions. The choreographer and designer work together in planning how a ballet should look.

Music for ballets

A choreographer may like to work with a composer, so that music is composed with a ballet in mind. The choreographer Wayne Eagling worked with the "pop" composer Vangelis on the synthesized music for Eagling's ballet, *Frankenstein*.

Alternatively, a choreographer will find a piece of music that inspires him or her. George Balanchine created his ballet *Violin Concerto* in response to the composer Stravinsky's violin concerto.

Sometimes existing pieces of music are arranged specially for new ballets. Composer Branwell Tovey arranged several pieces of Mussorgsky's music for David Bintley's ballet *Snow Queen*, so that all the steps fitted exactly.

Using steps in different ways

A ballet is similar to a piece of music. Sequences of steps are repeated and varied, just as tunes reoccur in a movement of music. Steps may be danced alone and then with a partner, just as different parts of the orchestra pick up and repeat a tune. The same step used differently can portray a variety of emotions.

First *arabesque en pointe*.

First *arabesque* on *demi-plié*.

Second *arabesque*.

A first *arabesque en pointe* can give the impression of strength and vitality, as danced by the Black Swan in the ballet *Swan Lake*. The same step looks much gentler on a *plié* with the foot flat. The step is used like this in the ballet *Giselle*.

Yet another mood is created by swapping the position of the arms and straightening the knee. A line is now formed along one side of the body creating a feeling of elegance or longing.

A *grand jeté* is a very dramatic leap through the air with legs outstretched. It can suggest different qualities, such as strength and exuberance. In *Coppélia*, Swanhilda leaps with her arms raised above her head, conveying joy and happiness.

Writing steps down

The art of recording a ballet or dance in a written code is called choreology. It is also sometimes called notation.

Before the skill was developed at the beginning of this century, ballets were only kept alive by constantly being danced. Some people attempted to keep written records of steps but these were often only understood by the writer. As a result, many ballets of the 19th century and earlier have been lost.

Nowadays most companies record, catalogue and store their ballets. This means a ballet can be staged by other companies throughout the world.

Dance notation

There are two methods of dance notation recognized throughout the ballet world.

One is called Labanotation, named after its inventor Rudolf von Laban.

The other is Benesh notation, named after Rudolf and Joan Benesh, who devised it.

Both methods can indicate any movement and position of the body and record whole ballets accurately.

Benesh notation

Benesh notation was developed in the late 1940s. Rudolf Benesh was an artist and Joan Benesh was a dancer. The idea for the code grew out of their joint desire to record movement on paper.

Nowadays dance students learn Benesh notation as part of their training. You can find out how Benesh notation works on the opposite page.

Labanotation

Laban devised Labanotation to record a style of movement which he began to develop in 1910. It is mainly used for contemporary dance.

What is a choreologist?

A person who records ballets is called a choreologist. Choreologists are trained dancers. They record new ballets as they are rehearsed and old ballets for future reference.

They may take early rehearsals of old ballets that are being restaged. They read the notated records and teach the dancers the steps.

Using video

Nowadays ballet companies usually make video recordings to support the work of the choreologist. While the notation records the steps of a ballet, the video records a particular interpretation of it.

Video is also used as a teaching device, helping dancers to learn a role.

How Benesh notation works

Like music, Benesh signs are written on a stave (five parallel lines).

They can be written on a sheet of music on a stave below the music. This means the movements can be read together with the music and shows how the steps correspond to it.

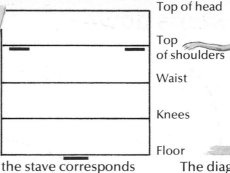

Positions are recorded by drawing dashes and other signs in an imaginary square on the stave. Each line of the stave corresponds to a different part of the body. Signs mark the exact spot occupied by the hands and feet.

The diagrams view the dancer from behind so signs on the left represent the dancer's left arm and leg.

The basic signs

— Level with body

| In front of body

● Behind body

Different signs show whether the hands and feet are in front or behind the body, or on a line level with it. The signs are shown above.

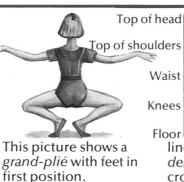

To show feet in fourth, right foot in front and arms as shown, you put an upright dash for the right foot and a dot for the left foot.

Dashes above the head and below the shoulder line represent the hands.

The feet

If feet are flat on the ground, the signs are below the base line. If they are *en pointe*, the signs go above the base line. Feet *en demi-pointe* (half point, or tiptoe) are indicated by signs through the base line. Feet together are shown by one long dash, rather than two separate ones.

Bending

✚ Level with body

✟ In front of body

✗ Behind body

A bent knee is indicated by a cross. There are three different types of cross depending on whether the knee is bent in front, behind or level with the body.

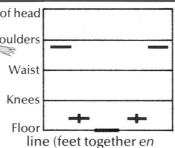

This picture shows a *grand-plié* with feet in first position.

To record it, you put a dash through the base line (feet together *en demi-pointe*) and crosses for the knees. Dashes show the position of the hands.

The arms

There is no need to record the slight curve of the arms which is natural in ballet. However, a big bend in an elbow is recorded with a cross, just like a knee bend. The type of cross you use depends on where the elbow is placed in relation to the rest of the body.

Continuous movement

Professional choreologists often need to record fast, continuous movement quickly. Instead of indicating a raise of the leg for example, by a series of dashes, which would take some time, they trace the path of the leg with one continuous line.

This diagram shows how a step called a *grand battement à la seconde* is recorded using a single line.

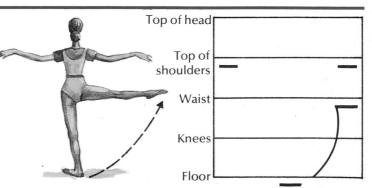

The structure of a ballet company

On these two pages you can see how a ballet company is made up and about the stages in a ballet dancer's career.

Most dancers start their careers by dancing in large groups. Those that show particular talent may be given small parts with solos to dance. Very few are ever good enough to dance the main parts in ballets.

The *corps de ballet*

The *corps de ballet* is a large group of dancers who perform together. In story ballets they dance as fairies, swans, village folk, courtiers and so on. In some Modern ballets they dance in group formations called *ensembles*.

Coryphées

Coryphée comes from the Greek word *koros* and means the leader of a chorus. In ballet, *coryphées* are the leaders of the *corps de ballet*. They may also play character roles or take small parts in story ballets.

Becoming a *coryphée* may be a step to becoming a soloist. However, some experienced dancers, who will never be soloists, are given the title in recognition of their skill.

In *The Sleeping Beauty*, fairy-tale characters like Red Riding Hood and the Wolf are *coryphées*.

Soloists

A soloist dances alone, or solo, in a ballet. He or she usually dances important but not leading roles.

In *The Sleeping Beauty*, the Fairy of Modesty dances a solo when she brings a gift for the christening of Princess Aurora (the Sleeping Beauty). In *Swan Lake* a soloist dances the part of the Black Swan, the evil swan queen.

Very few dancers reach the level of soloist.

Principals

A principal is someone who dances a leading role in a ballet. For example, in *Swan Lake*, Prince Siegfried is the male principal role and Odette, the princess in the guise of a swan, is the female principal role.

Senior principals, who are older members of the company, usually take important character roles. These may be physically less demanding yet require great skill in interpreting the characters. The Ugly Sisters in *Cinderella* are played by senior male principals.

A principal ballerina is sometimes called a *prima ballerina*. The male equivalent is *premier danseur* but the term is rarely used.

Behind the scenes

This section is about the people who work backstage, alongside the dancers. It tells you about their jobs and describes how everyone works together to make the day to day running of a company go smoothly.

Artistic director

The artistic director plans what ballets will be performed and decides who will dance each role. He or she also employs choreographers to create new ballets. Most ballet companies have at least one full-time choreographer.

Teachers and physiotherapists

Most companies have a ballet master or mistress to rehearse ballets and supervise the *corps de ballet*. A *répétiteur* also rehearses ballets. One or two teachers take daily classes and give individual coaching.

A physiotherapist treats dancers' injuries.

Wardrobe

In the Wardrobe department, a wardrobe master looks after male costumes and a wardrobe mistress takes care of female costumes. Wardrobe assistants wash and repair outfits. There is also a wig master or mistress, who is often a trained hairdresser.

Orchestra

A ballet company has its own orchestra. The conductor and members of the orchestra work under a musical director who is in charge of music for ballets, rehearsals and classes. The conductor rehearses the orchestra and is responsible for their playing.

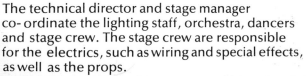

Stage management

The technical director and stage manager co-ordinate the lighting staff, orchestra, dancers and stage crew. The stage crew are responsible for the electrics, such as wiring and special effects, as well as the props.

The timing and positioning of each member of the *corps de ballet* must be perfect, or the whole effect looks ragged.

A female dancer of soloist or principal status can be given the title of ballerina.

It takes years of hard work to become a principal. Only those with exceptional talent, a brilliant technique and perfect physique ever succeed.

Publicity

A press officer stays in contact with the press, informing them of future performances.

A marketing officer commissions posters, leaflets and programmes advertising ballets.*

Some companies have an education or outreach officer, who builds up new audiences by working in schools and the community.

Choreologists and archivists

Most companies have a choreologist to record and teach ballets. They also employ an archivist who collects photos, programmes and press cuttings relating to the company.

Administration

The administrative director is responsible for major policy decisions which can affect the company's public image. Administrative assistants and clerical staff carry out the decisions.

A company also has a general manager who arranges tours, salaries and general business matters.

*You can find out more about publicity on page 17.

Putting on a ballet

Putting a ballet on stage involves an enormous amount of work from many different people. On these two pages you can find out who is involved and what they do.

Dancers rehearsing a ballet.

The dancers

Dancers start rehearsing a new ballet at least six months before its first performance. An existing ballet is prepared for the stage in a matter of weeks.

Schedules for rehearsals are displayed on "call sheets".

CALL SHEET

Usually four people learn each part. Roles like Princess Aurora in *The Sleeping Beauty* are too demanding for one person to dance every night, so dancers take it in turns. If a principal is ill, young dancers may get the chance to make their début.

The orchestra

To begin with, the orchestra rehearse the music separately from the dancers. When the dancers are familiar with their steps, they rehearse with the orchestra. The musicians have to get used to changes in tempo (speed) which different parts of the ballet demand.

The set and costumes

The set (the scenery on the stage) and costumes* play a major part in creating the atmosphere of a ballet. They are worked out by a designer in conversation with the choreographer.

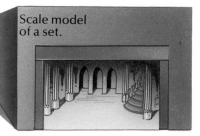

Scale model of a set.

The background scene may be painted on to a backcloth or it may be made out of wood, with windows and doors through which dancers can enter and leave.

To get an idea of the overall effect of a set before it is built, an accurate scale model may be built.

Lighting

Stage lights are hung above the stage and in the auditorium. They can create impressions such as a sunrise or sunset. In *Petrushka*, blue lights are used to give the impression of a Russian winter.

The arrangement of lights above the stage is called the rig.

*You can find out more about costumes on pages 18-19.

The publicity department

The marketing officer has posters printed to advertise a ballet. They are displayed where lots of people will see them, such as in libraries and stations, from four or five weeks before performances start. Advertisements are placed in newspapers and magazines.

Last rehearsals

From about two weeks before the first night (first performance), the dancers rehearse on stage to get used to its size. On the day before the first performance there is a full "dress rehearsal". Dancers wear their costumes and perform as if to an audience.

What happens backstage?

The cast must be backstage half an hour before the performance begins. First they put on their make-up.* Then they do their hair. A wig mistress helps to fit wigs and a dresser helps the cast into their costumes. The dancers put their ballet shoes on last. They may glue them to their tights to make them extra secure.

On stage

Stage manager

Wings →

The stage manager runs the show from a "prompt" corner.

Orchestra pit

Fifteen minutes before the performance, the orchestra take their place in the "pit" and tune their instruments.

When the stage manager signals for the auditorium lights to go down, the orchestra begins the music and the stage manager gives the "curtain up" signal.

The music is relayed to the dressing room, so dancers know when they are due on stage.

On tour

Most companies spend a good part of a year on tour in their own country and abroad. Their programme is worked out at least a year in advance.

Everything travels with the company: costumes, scenery, lights and even office equipment.

The ballet La Fille Mal Gardée has a small white pony in the cast. This would travel with the company along with its owner to care for it.

Everything is packed into huge lorries. Each dancer's make-up and practice costumes are stored in individual boxes, called "blue boxes".

For a three month tour, about 30 pairs of satin *pointe* shoes are carried on tour for each female dancer and 18 pairs for each male dancer.

The wardrobe staff take washing machines, tumble driers and crates containing sewing equipment.

*You can find out more about make-up over the page.

Costumes and make-up

Designing and making costumes is an art in itself. They help to create the mood of a ballet. As well as looking right, they must be light and easy to move in. Dancers often wear bits of old costume in rehearsals to help them get the feel of the ballet.

Hairstyles and make-up also help to conjure up weird and wonderful characters.

Different kinds of costume

Three different types of female costume reflect the Romantic, Classical and Modern movements in ballet. Fashion and social changes have had less effect on male costumes than on female costumes.

Classic costume.

Romantic costume.

The costume for a Romantic ballerina is a fairy-like, calf-length dress, usually white, with a fitted bodice and floaty sleeves. For fairy characters, wings may be attached to the shoulders.

The *tutu,* a short ballet dress with a tight bodice and layers of sticking out frills, is characteristic of Classical ballets.

Many Modern ballets are danced in simple, light dresses, or Greek-style tunics. All-over body tights are also worn by women and men. They are dyed and decorated in lots of different ways.

In Modern ballets, a dancer's hair may be worn in almost any style. It may be loose and natural or worn with a head-dress.

Male dancers usually wear tights. This is so the audience can see their legs executing the steps. In some Romantic and Classical ballets, men have to look like princes, so they wear tunics.

In Modern ballets, men's costumes are more varied. In the ballet *Enigma Variations,* the dancers wear ordinary trousers.

Character costumes

Many costumes help to portray a character. In *The Prodigal Son,* Balanchine's ballet of the parable from the Bible, the son wears a jewelled, Roman-style costume. This conveys his lavish spending and his rebellion against his Jewish family.

In the film ballet *The Tales of Beatrix Potter,* the dancers wear masks right over their heads to make them look like animals.

Some costumes express a theme or a spirit, such as the Spirit of the Rose in the ballet *Le Spectre de la Rose,* first danced by Nijinsky in 1911.

Prodigal son.

Mr Jeremy Fisher in *The Tales of Beatrix Potter.*

The Spirit of the Rose.

Making costumes

Costume designers make detailed sketches of their ideas. Sometimes they attach samples of possible fabrics. They have to remember that bright stage lights may distort colours and textures.

Jewellery is made of light, fake materials which gleam under the spotlights.

Mouse costume.

The costumes are made by skilled dressmakers and tailors. *Tutus* are especially hard to make.

Costumes must never restrict the dancers, so sleeves have to allow the arms to move freely. Fastenings consist of hooks and eyes instead of zips, so the dancers feel secure in them.

A *tutu* takes at least two days to make.

Make-up

Make-up is worn to accentuate the dancers' features so their faces can be seen under strong stage lighting. Eyes especially need to be highlighted.

Close up, stage make-up looks overdone. When seen by the audience it looks perfectly natural.

Make-up can also be used to create a character, such as a clown. Dancers use "nose-putty" to make false noses and chins. Careful highlighting can change the shape of a face and alter eyebrow shapes. Lines and smudges are painted on to look like wrinkles.

These pictures show a male dancer transforming himself into one of the Ugly Sisters in the ballet *Cinderella*.

1. A false plastic nose is glued on with special gum called spirit gum. ▶

2. Make-up exaggerates ▼ the lips and eyes and creates haughty, arched eyebrows.

Period costumes

Costumes may be designed to suggest a particular period in history.

Costumes for *Romeo and Juliet* were like 16th century Renaissance clothes to fit in with the period in which the story is set.

◀ 3. Sticks of greasepaint (special stage make-up) are used to shade and highlight the face, creating wrinkles and warts.

Making expressions

These expressions can be created by making up the eyes in different ways.

Mournful

Eyebrows and outer corners of eyes slope down. Dots at inner corners are put high up.

Fierce

Eyebrows are thickened and tilted up. Shading at the sides makes eyes look smaller. Wrinkles are painted between eyebrows.

Mild, simple

Eyebrows are arched and eyes enlarged.

Watching a ballet

Before you go to see a ballet, find out as much as you can about it. For instance, you could borrow a record of the music from a record library.

Buy a programme before the performance. This sets out the ballet's story or theme.

You can buy tickets from the theatre's box office or you can ask to be put on their mailing list. They will then send you details of future events. You return a form with money for ballets you want to see.

The *corps de ballet*.

In many Modern ballets the dancers make unusual shapes, like this.

Story ballets unfold with a mixture of dance and mime (see opposite). In some ballets the story is interrupted by set pieces of choreography when two or three people perform together. The *corps de ballet* dance together in group formations.

Ballets without a definite story have meaning, too. The dancers use all sorts of shapes and movements to express moods and reactions. If you look carefully, you may be able to understand what the dancers are saying with their bodies.

Steps to look out for

Here are some of the most difficult and exciting steps to look out for when you go to see a ballet.
Watch for changes in the speed of dancing, too.

Slow, gentle sections follow fast, vigorous ones. Group dances may follow solos. Sections are repeated or changed slightly to form a pattern.

Barrel turn
The barrel turn is also known as a *coupe jeté en tournant*.

Fish dive

Bourrées

Temps de poisson

The barrel turn, usually performed by a man, is a spectacular curving jump, followed by a quick turn on the ground. Some Russian dancers lean over so far that they are almost parallel with the floor.

A fish dive is performed by a male and female dancer. The male dancer catches the ballerina on his thigh as she swoops to the floor in a graceful, curving shape, like a fish darting through water.

Bourrées are performed *en pointe*. The dancer makes a series of tiny opening and closing steps. This gives the impression of gliding. It enables the dancer to travel across the stage very quickly.

The *temps de poisson* (fish step) is another fishlike movement. The dancer jumps in the air arching his body sideways like a sinuous, leaping fish.
This step is rarely performed by women.

Mime

Mime is a set of gestures which have a particular meaning and so help to tell a story. Some gestures are like the ones deaf people use.

In ballet there are over 200 mime gestures. They occur mostly in older ballets, such as *The Nutcracker*. However, the character Lise performs a mime in the Modern ballet, *La Fille Mal Gardée*. Here are some mime gestures you can look out for.

Beg

Love

Plead

Protect

Incline your body forward, right arm outstretched and left arm slightly in front.

Cradle your heart with both hands and incline your head slightly towards the left.

Place the palms of both hands together as if in prayer and incline your body forward.

Throw both arms back and hold your head high. Your body should face the danger.

You

Shoot

Death

Fear

Point your right hand towards the character concerned and face him or her.

Raise your arms and hands as if using a bow and arrow and look upwards.

Extend your hands and arms and cross them in front of your body, with fists lightly clenched.

Turn away from danger, raise left arm over your head and shield your face with right palm.

Famous theatres and companies

The Bolshoi Theatre.

Most dancers dream of performing in theatres such as the Royal Opera House in London, the Bolshoi Theatre in Moscow, the Metropolitan Opera House in New York and the Sydney Opera House.

Nowadays most major ballet companies travel abroad to dance in each other's theatres. This gives people in many countries the opportunity of seeing famous companies from all over the world.

Choosing your seat

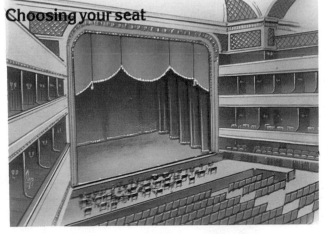

The best seats are usually in the centre of the auditorium and are slightly raised so you can see the dancers clearly. At the very front it is difficult to see the dancers' feet. The cheapest seats are usually high up in the gallery. From here you get a good overall view of the patterns the dancers make.

Some theatres run clubs for young people to join. Members can attend rehearsals and meet dancers.

Ballet as a career

Ballet can be an exciting and glamorous career but it is difficult to get into.

It is also a short career. The demands ballet makes upon the body mean that in their mid-30s most dancers have to take up other careers. Some become ballet teachers or critics.* Others become make-up artists or stage managers or retrain for totally different careers, such as accountancy.

Qualities you need

Well-shaped head.

Long neck.

Slim.

Neither too tall nor too small.

Well proportioned.

Strong arches neither too flat nor too high.

Strong feet.

As well as a good physique, a ballet dancer needs a sense of rhythm, a feeling for music, a good memory, an ability to accept correction and determination to work hard. Another important quality is a desire to bring pleasure to an audience.

Ballet training

You can start proper ballet classes at the age of seven. At ten or eleven, talented students may go to a full-time ballet school.**

Many promising students continue at an ordinary school until they are 16 or 17, taking ballet classes in their spare time.

Exam pass certificate.

An alternative is to go to a vocational school. Students get a broad theatrical training including acting, mime, ballet, modern dance, tap and folk dance as well as a general education.

Wherever you train you can take exams to mark your progress.

Further training

At about the age of 15 you will probably decide whether you want to become a professional ballet dancer, follow another career in the theatre or just continue ballet for fun.

If you want to become a professional ballet dancer you must train for at least two years at a full-time ballet school attached to a company. Such schools take students from the ages of 15 or 16.

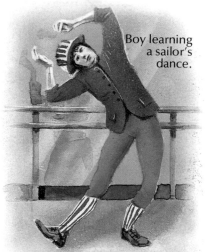

Boy learning a sailor's dance.

As well as practising the basics, you learn how to dance with a partner and how to dance character roles. You learn some contemporary and folk dance and pieces from ballets to perform at auditions and to prepare you for joining a company. This helps build the confidence you need for a professional career.

Most ballet schools, for instance the Royal Ballet School in London or the New York Ballet School, are attached to a company. This means the company has a constant supply of new talent.

This also gives the students the chance to perform in small walk-on roles or in the back row of the *corps de ballet*. The professional experience is valuable for the students' careers.

22 *A ballet critic is somone who reviews ballets in books and newspapers.
**You can find out about life at a ballet school on pages 24-25.

Joining a company

At the end of the training, a graduation performance takes place. The director of the company attends and picks out the most promising dancers to join the company.

The company may need to fill a vacancy during the year. The director watches classes and selects a dancer, usually after consultation with the ballet master or mistress.

If you do not manage to get into a major company you can apply to smaller companies at home or companies abroad. Write round asking to be seen and then audition until you get a job.

Alternative careers

You may have to give up the idea of being a classical ballet dancer, perhaps because you have not got all the specific qualities ballet demands. It could also be because you have grown too much or had an injury.

Whatever the reason, you may want to look for an alternative career.

One possibility for people who love performing is to work in the theatre. Some ballet dancers find they prefer this. For instance, the English dancer, Wayne Sleep, has moved from ballet to acting and singing.

Becoming part of the dance scene in the theatrical world is very different from joining a ballet company. The dancers must audition for every job and be able to dance in many different styles, including tap and jazz.

There are also opportunities in theatre and dance companies for those who wish to pursue theatre design, choreography and directing.

Another possibility is to change to contemporary dance. Many classically trained dancers prefer to work in this less rigid style. It is also useful because dancers do not have to conform to a stereotyped shape.

Ex-ballet dancer teaching choreology.

Many dancers turn to teaching at some stage in their career. They might teach in a full-time ballet school or start their own ballet classes.

If you decide early on that you want to teach, some ballet schools train people specially to teach ballet and dance. You can take exams to become a qualified ballet teacher.

Academic training

Nowadays you can study ballet and dance at polytechnics or universities. These courses cover the theory and history of dance as well as giving practical dance or ballet tuition.

With this sort of qualification you can teach ballet and dance in ordinary schools or the community.

It is unusual to join a ballet company after such a course, though some people join a contemporary company.

23

Life at a ballet school

If you show promise and have the right physique, you may begin full-time ballet school at the age of 11. Students come from all over the country and some from abroad, so many of them board at the school.

Despite the hard work and discipline expected of ballet students, competition to get a place is stiff and the selection procedure is tough.

Getting into ballet school

You can apply for an audition at the age of 11 even if you have never been to a ballet class. What is important is your physique and ability to express yourself in dance.

A group of examiners will watch you do simple exercises. They may ask you to make up a dance to music, to test the power of your imagination.

You will also be given a medical examination to check your fitness. In order to find out how much you are likely to grow, your hands are X-rayed. Girls must not grow too tall and boys must not be too small, as in classical ballet boys need to be taller than their partners.

The width of the dark gaps between the bones of the wrist show how much growth is ahead. The hand on the left has wide gaps which means a lot of growth is ahead.

Ballet classes

At first you spend about one and a half hours doing ballet. This increases as you move up the school. The classes are small and boys and girls are taught separately.

To begin with you concentrate on technique. As placing the parts of the body becomes automatic, you learn short dances, or *enchaînements,* at the end of the class.

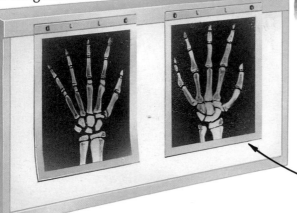

When girls are 11 or 12 they start to go up *en pointe*. At first this is only done for a few minutes at the end of every class.

Gradually, more time is spent *en pointe* so after two years pupils do about an hour's *pointe* work a day.

You should not go *en pointe* until your teacher thinks you are ready. There is more about *pointe* work on page 39.

Boys' training is quite athletic. They use weights to build strength. When they have done this for at least a year, they take classes with girls, learning to partner but not yet lift them.

24

Theatre craft and choreography

Dancers wearing special character costumes.

Alongside ballet technique, other important aspects of ballet are taught, such as theatre craft. This tells you how to project yourself to an audience and convey different moods and emotions.

Students learn character dances from ballets and some folk and national dances. They wear special shoes for character dancing.

The students also have choreography classes. They may create their own dances or experiment with steps, putting them together to make interesting patterns.

Sometimes they may choose a particular theme and make up a dance to reflect it.

Choreology

Another skill you learn is choreology (see pages 12-13). You may use it in class for learning the steps of dances.

Other classes

As well as ballet classes, students do ordinary lessons. Some subjects, such as music, French and biology are stressed. Human biology helps students understand the skeleton and how muscles work.

Assessments

Each student's progress is regularly checked. These checks are called assessments. Pupils may be asked to leave the school if their dancing is not quite good enough or if they have grown too much or too little. As few students ever reach the top in ballet, they are always taught to look positively at alternatives to ballet.

(see pages 12-13)

Training round the world

Russia

The Kirov Ballet in Leningrad and the Bolshoi Ballet in Moscow have their own schools. Russian training is famous for teaching dancers to use their backs expressively, for instance, when doing spectacular leaps.

Denmark

The Royal Danish Ballet School is famous for a style established by a teacher called Auguste Bournonville. This style enables dancers to jump in a particularly bouncy way and is renowned for its neat footwork.

France

The Paris Opéra School is attached to the Opéra Company where many great dancers have made their début. Students are called *les petits rats* (the little rats)!

America

Training at the New York City Ballet School follows the style established by the founder of the company, George Balanchine. The style is swift and dramatic.

Britain

London's Royal Ballet School was originally started to supply new talent to the Royal Ballet Company. Today its pupils go on to dance with companies all over the world, as well as with the Royal Ballet.

Canada and Australia

Both the Canadian National Ballet and the Australian Ballet were founded by former members of London's Royal Ballet. Training is similar to that in Britain, though the National School in Toronto has developed a particularly lively style of ballet.

Exercises at the *barre*

On the next few pages there are some simple exercises for you to try. All the exercises follow the Cecchetti technique (see page 7). You might do them at a class and you can practise them at home.

On these two pages are some *barre* exercises. At home you can hold on to the back of a chair. At the *barre*, you usually practise an exercise in one direction and then turn round and practise facing the other way. This exercises both sides of your body equally.

Make sure that you always hold your spine and head very straight.

The elbow of your free arm must not droop. Hold your fingers gracefully. There are five positions of the arms. You can find out what they are on the opposite page.

Your toes on the floor should be long and straight. If you stand incorrectly your toes will curl up in order to grip the floor.

How far you stand from the *barre* is very important because it affects how you place your body. The hand on the *barre* should be slightly in front of your body and you should be able to imagine a straight line running down the middle of you.

If you stand too far away from or too close to the *barre*, this imaginary line will be distorted. Experiment to find the best position for you.

Plié is from the French verb *plier* meaning to bend.

Pliés

*Pliés** are a good warming up exercise because they stretch all the muscles of your legs and prepare them for the later exercises. They also help you to achieve good turn-out.

There are two types of *pliés*: *grands pliés* (full knee bends) and *demi-pliés* (half knee bends).

Demi-pliés are especially good for stretching the tendons at the backs of your heels.

You can do *pliés* in all five positions of the feet (see pages 6-7). At first, practise them facing the *barre* with your feet in first and second position.

Demi-pliés

To do a *demi-plié*, face the *barre*. Rest both hands on it and put your feet in first position. ▶

Grands pliés

With *grands pliés*, you start in the same position as a *demi-plié*, with your feet in first position. ▶

Battements tendus

Battements tendus literally means stretched beatings. They stretch and strengthen the arch underneath your foot.

In this exercise you point your foot to the front, side, back and side again. The pictures show the exercise to the front and side.

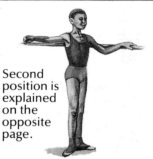

Second position is explained on the opposite page.

Put your feet in first position with your legs well turned out and your arm in second position. ▶

Battements glissés

Glissé comes from the French verb *glisser* and means gliding.

In this exercise you slide your foot along the ground and lift it. It helps to develop swift footwork. You do this exercise to the front, side, back and to the side again. Here it is done to the side.

Put your feet in first position and place your arm in fifth *en bas* (see next page). ▶

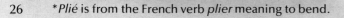

When you go down, don't "sit" on your hips. Lift up out of them when you rise up.

Bend your knees as far as they will go without letting your heels come off the floor.

Slowly straighten your knees, taking the same amount of time to rise as you took to go down.

Demi-plié in second position.

In a *demi-plié* in second position, you should feel the weight between your feet, not on your feet.

Do not pull on the *barre*.

Bend your knees, keeping your heels on the floor until you have to let them lift smoothly off it.

Now begin to rise slowly, first replacing your heels on the floor and then straightening your knees.

Grand plié in second position.

To do a *grand plié* in second, you must not lift your heels. Keep them firmly on the floor.

Point your toe and turn your leg out.

Stretch your right leg in front to fourth position. Then slide your foot back to close in first postion.

Now stretch your right leg to the side to second position. Keep your body and hips straight.

Bring your right leg back to first position. Repeat the exercise to the back and to the side again.

Do this to the front, side, back and side again.

Slide your foot along the ground to second. Lift it 5-7cm (2-3in) off the ground with toes pointed.

Now lower the toes to the floor to second position. Remember not to let your hips twist to the side.

Finally, slide your toes along the floor back to first position, gradually replacing your heel.

The positions of the arms

These positions follow the Cecchetti technique. They are the basic positions, though later on you will use your arms in many different ways.

First position

Second position

Demi-seconde

Third position

Fourth position

En haut

En avant

Fifth position

En bas

En haut

En avant

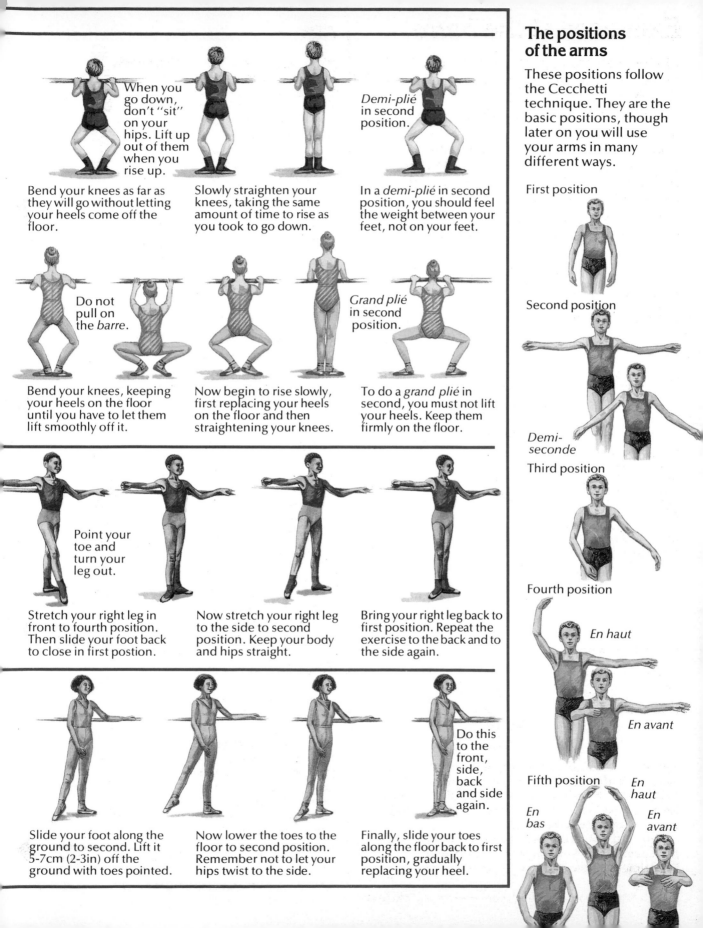

Rondes de jambe à terre

Here are some more exercises at the *barre*, starting with *rondes de jambe à terre*. This means circles of the leg on the ground. You mark out a semi-circle with your foot. It is an excellent way to loosen up your hip ligaments and improve turn-out. When you start the semi-circle at the front, it is called *en dehors*. When you start it at the back it is called *en dedans*. The pictures on the right show a *ronde de jambe en dehors*.

The exercises on these two pages are shown using the right foot. When you do them, repeat them with your left foot. There are some hints on pointing and positioning your feet on the far right.

Put your feet in first position and your right arm in second position.

Slide your right foot forward to fourth, pointing your toes.

Battements frappés

Frappé comes from the French verb *frapper* which means to strike. In *battements frappés*, you cross your heel alternately in front and behind your supporting leg and strike the floor with your foot. This exercise should be performed with quick movements and is very good for sharpening your responses. It is a good preparation for jumping steps later.

A similar step to try is called *petits battements sur le cou-de-pied*. You can find out how to do it at the end of the row of pictures on the right.

Arm in second position.

Right heel resting on ankle bone.

Bend your right knee and cross your heel in front of your left anklebone. This is the starting position.

Sharply move your right foot down and out so the ball of your foot strikes the floor at the side.

Grands battements

Grands battements means large beats. You raise your pointed foot from the ground, keeping both legs straight. This strengthens the legs and increases your extension (how high you can stretch them).

Like all other exercises at the *barre* you can perform *grands battements* to the front, side, back and to the side again. This is called *en croix*, meaning in the shape of a cross. These pictures show a *grand battement* to the front. You can do them with your feet starting in and returning to either first or fifth position.

Place your feet in first position and your right arm in second.

Point your right foot in front of you in fourth position.

Développés

The name of this exercise means, as it sounds, developments. *Développés* are slow movements in which the leg is slowly extended to the highest point possible. The pictures on the right show a *développé* to the front. When you practise them, do them *en croix*, that is, to the front, side, back and to the side again.

Développés help you to learn control of your leg as it unfolds and to produce a beautiful line with your body. The movement should be done gradually and smoothly.

Stand up straight with your knees pulled up tightly.

Put your feet in fifth position and your right arm in fifth *en bas* (see previous page).

Point your right foot and gradually slide it up your leg to your knee. Keep both legs turned out.

Do not twist your hips. Keep them level throughout the exercise.

Then slide your toes around on the floor to point to second position.

Next, slide your toes round to point to fourth position at the back.

Finally, slide your foot along the floor back to first position.

Tips on pointing your feet

Foot pointing to the front.

When you point your foot to the front, your leg should be turned out from the hip. Your heel should be held up, with the big toe touching the ground, not the little one. Your foot should be in line with your leg straight in front of you.

Your toes should be about 7cm (3in) off the ground.

When your foot leaves the floor after the strike, point it. At the same time tighten your knee.

Bend your right knee again and bring your right heel to the back of your left anklebone.

Petits battements sur le cou-de-pied

The name of this step means little beats on the ankle.

You alternately cross your outside heel in front and behind your inside ankle bone. Keep the ball of your foot on the floor and your foot flexed (not pointed).

Foot pointing to the side.

When you point to the side, again make sure your foot is in line with your leg. Lift the heel and point the tips of your toes. Rest them only very lightly on the ground. Don't twist your heel backwards.

Keep your inside leg straight with your knee pulled tight.

Then lift your right leg as high as possible, keeping both your hips in line.

Next, lower your right foot to the floor back to fourth position.

Finally, slide your right foot back to first without bending your knee.

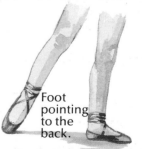

Foot pointing to the back.

At the back, rest lightly on the inside of your big toe and press your heel down. Don't turn your foot in as this will make your heel stick up in the air.

En l'air

As you slide your pointed foot towards your knee, smoothly raise your right arm in front of you.

Then slowly unfold your leg in front of you. This position is called *en l'air*, meaning in the air.

Straighten your leg out fully. At the same time, open your arm out to second position.

Centre work

In the second half of a ballet class you move away from the *barre* into the centre of the room. Here you repeat some of the exercises you have already done but without the *barre* to aid your balance.

Then you move on to specific centre work such as exercises for *port de bras* - the way you move your arms smoothly from one position to another. You also learn how to do steps such as the *arabesque* (shown opposite) and *allegro* (quick) steps. There are some *allegro* steps for you to try over the page.

In centre work there are eight basic positions you can use which show off the line of your body to best advantage from different angles. You can find out what they are below.

The eight positions of the body

A la quatrième derrière (in fourth behind).

A la seconde (in second).

A la quatrième devant (in fourth in front).

Ecarté (thrown open).

Croisé devant (crossed in front).

Croisé derrière (crossed behind).

Epaulé (shouldered).

Effacé (turned away).

The eight positions or directions of the body form the basis of many of the movements in ballet. You will use them every time you do exercises in the centre. They are designed so that the audience see a clear outline of your body whatever direction you are facing.

Try out the eight positions yourself. The name of each position is shown next to it with its English translation in brackets.

Ports de bras

Ports de bras means carriage of the arms. They are exercises which teach you to move your arms in a graceful, flowing way.

Try the simple arm exercises on the right. Before you start, make sure you are standing up straight with your shoulders down.

Relax your arms, with the elbows and wrists slightly bent so your arms make a smooth curve. Your fingers should feel long and extended, but not tense.

Feet in fifth position.

Raise your arms from fifth *en bas* to fifth *en avant*. (See page 27.)

Then smoothly open your arms out wide to second position.

Now take your arms back down through first position to fifth *en bas*.

Feet and arms in fifth.

Incline your head to your lower arm.

Incline your head to your lower arm.

Raise your right arm to fifth *en avant* and your left arm to *demi-seconde*.

Swap the position of your arms passing them through second position.

Lower both arms to fifth *en bas* passing the left arm through *demi-seconde*.

Arabesques

An *arabesque* is a well-known ballet position. It looks quite easy but it is difficult to do because it needs considerable control and balance.

You balance on one leg with your other leg stretched out behind you. Your arms can be in various positions but they must make a shape which compliments the position of the legs.

The pictures show you how to reach first *arabesque* through *développé à la seconde* and then how to move from first to second *arabesque*.

Arms in fifth *en bas*.

Raise arms to fifth *en avant*.

Open arms out to second

Stand with your feet in fifth. Gradually bend your right leg to the side.

Pointing your right foot, slide it to your left knee and unfold your leg.

Now extend your right leg out to the side (*à la seconde*).

Turn palms downwards and extend the fingers.

Left heel slightly forward.

This is the first *arabesque* position.

This is the second *arabesque* position.

Turn your body sideways so your right leg is behind you. Turn both feet out.

Raise your left hand to eye level and slightly lower your right arm.

Now swap the position of your arms, passing them through second position.

Adage steps

Slow, sustained movements such as the *arabesque* are called *adage* steps. *Adage* comes from the Italian *ad agio* meaning at ease.

When you do *adage* steps you should concentrate on developing grace, balance and "line". Line refers to the flowing curves which your body makes. These smooth, graceful lines are characteristic of the harmony and balance of classical ballet.

Another common *adage* step is the *attitude*. In this step, you raise your leg behind your body, curving it by bending and lifting the knee.

Glissades

Glissades are gliding steps. You travel sideways by sliding your feet along the ground to your right, left, forwards or backwards. Make them as smooth as possible.

Start slowly and build up speed as you find them easier.

Stand with your feet in fifth and your arms in fifth *en bas* (low).

Widen your arms to first position.

Demi-plié and then slide your right foot along the ground.

Now raise your foot, pointed, to about 7cm (3in) above the ground.

▶

Pas de bourrées

In music, a *bourrée* is a dance done to a certain beat. In ballet, there are a variety of *bourrées*.

The step on the right is one of the first you will learn. It is called a *pas de bourrée en avant* (to the front).

You do this step facing the *effacé* direction. (This is explained on page 30.)

Left leg in front.

Open your arms to *demi-seconde*.

Foot about 7cm (3in) from ground.

Rising up on tip-toe is called *relevé*.

Face the *effacé* direction and place your feet and arms in fifth position.

Do a *demi-plié* on your left leg. Slide your right leg to the side and raise it.

Bring your right leg to close in fifth and rise up on tip-toe on both legs.

▶

Pirouettes

A *pirouette*, meaning a whirl, is a step where you spin on one leg. Here you can see how to do a *pirouette en dehors*. This is quite a simple step.

When turning, dancers use a special technique called "spotting" to prevent them getting giddy. You can find out more about it below.

Focus on a point straight ahead.

Stand with your feet in fifth position, left leg in front. Place your arms in fifth *en bas*.

Point your left leg to the side and pass your arms through fifth *en avant* to second positon.

Bend your right knee and bring your left heel to the back of your right ankle. Bring your arms to third.

▶

How to "spot"

Dancers have to learn how to "spot", that is, to focus on an object while turning or spinning in a *pirouette*.

In class, you learn to spot by looking at a fixed point on the wall. You focus on it for as long as possible during a turn before flicking your head round to look at it again.

Many theatres have a small, blue light especially for dancers on the stage to focus on. It is usually set very high up at the back of the auditorium.

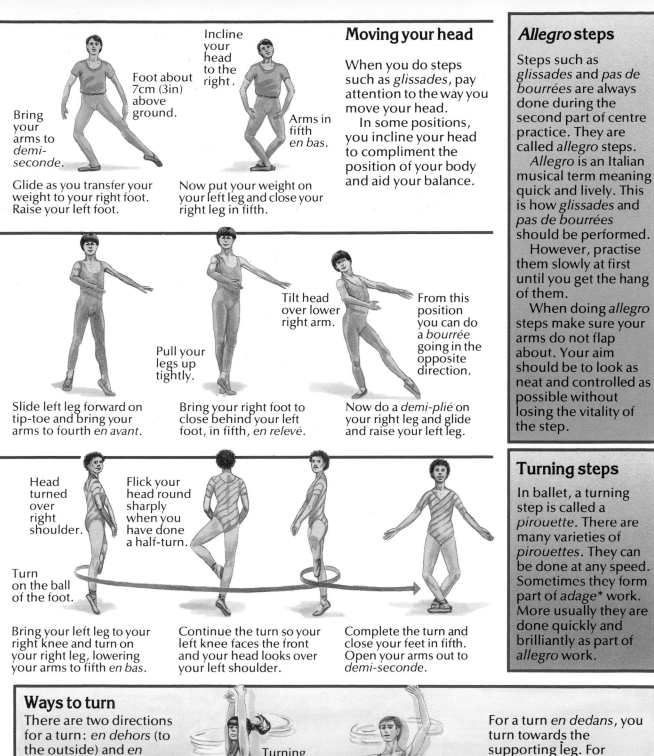

Bring your arms to *demi-seconde*.

Foot about 7cm (3in) above ground.

Glide as you transfer your weight to your right foot. Raise your left foot.

Incline your head to the right.

Arms in fifth *en bas*.

Now put your weight on your left leg and close your right leg in fifth.

Moving your head

When you do steps such as *glissades*, pay attention to the way you move your head.

In some positions, you incline your head to compliment the position of your body and aid your balance.

Allegro steps

Steps such as *glissades* and *pas de bourrées* are always done during the second part of centre practice. They are called *allegro* steps.

Allegro is an Italian musical term meaning quick and lively. This is how *glissades* and *pas de bourrées* should be performed.

However, practise them slowly at first until you get the hang of them.

When doing *allegro* steps make sure your arms do not flap about. Your aim should be to look as neat and controlled as possible without losing the vitality of the step.

Slide left leg forward on tip-toe and bring your arms to fourth *en avant*.

Pull your legs up tightly.

Tilt head over lower right arm.

Bring your right foot to close behind your left foot, in fifth, *en relevé*.

From this position you can do a *bourrée* going in the opposite direction.

Now do a *demi-plié* on your right leg and glide and raise your left leg.

Head turned over right shoulder.

Turn on the ball of the foot.

Bring your left leg to your right knee and turn on your right leg, lowering your arms to fifth *en bas*.

Flick your head round sharply when you have done a half-turn.

Continue the turn so your left knee faces the front and your head looks over your left shoulder.

Complete the turn and close your feet in fifth. Open your arms out to *demi-seconde*.

Turning steps

In ballet, a turning step is called a *pirouette*. There are many varieties of *pirouettes*. They can be done at any speed. Sometimes they form part of *adage** work. More usually they are done quickly and brilliantly as part of *allegro* work.

Ways to turn

There are two directions for a turn: *en dehors* (to the outside) and *en dedans* (to the inside). For a turn *en dehors* you turn away from your supporting leg. For example, if you are standing on your right leg, you lift your left leg and turn to the left.

Turning *en attitude*.

For a turn *en dedans*, you turn towards the supporting leg. For instance you stand on your right leg, lift the left leg and turn to the right. You can turn *en arabesque* (with your leg stretched behind you) or *en attitude* (with your leg curved round behind you).

Adage comes from the Italian musical term *adagio*, meaning slow.

Jumps and travelling steps

In the last part of a class you do jumps and travelling steps. There are two types: *petit allegro* (small and fast) and *grand allegro* (big and slower).

Jumps begin and end with a *demi-plié*. This helps you spring off the ground and land without jarring your joints.

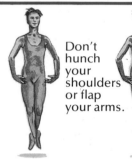

When landing from a jump, the tips of your toes should touch the ground first. Your sole should touch the ground next and lastly your heel. This makes the landing smooth and quiet.

Changements

A *changement* is a jump in which you change the position of your feet before landing. Its name means changing. You can see how to do them on the right.

As you progress you may learn how to do *changements battus,* where you beat your legs together in the air before changing them.

Hold your arms in fifth *en bas.*

Don't hunch your shoulders or flap your arms.

Put your feet in fifth, right foot in front. Then *demi-plié*, keeping your heels on the ground.

Now jump straight up into the air with your legs straight and your toes pointed.

Change your legs in the air and land in a *demi-plié* in fifth position, this time with your left foot in front.

Entrechats

An *entrechat* is a step where you jump straight up in the air and change the position of your feet a number of times before landing. This is called "beating" your feet.

Entrechats are often combined with other steps and jumps.

On the right, you can find out how to do an *entrechat quatre.*

Arms in fifth *en bas.*

Keep your legs very slightly bent.

From a *demi-plié* in fifth position, right foot in front, spring into the air. As you jump, push your feet downwards.

While you are in the air, change the position of your legs very quickly so that your left leg is now in front of your right.

Before you land from the jump, change your legs back so you finish in a *demi-plié* in fifth, with your right leg in front.

Record breaking *entrechats*

The dancer Wayne Sleep has performed an *entrechat dix*, crossing and recrossing his legs five times before landing.

The Russian dancer Nijinsky is said to have done an *entrechat douze*, crossing his legs six times.

Wayne Sleep's achievement is in the Guinness Book of Records.

Pas de chats

A *pas de chat* (step of a cat) is a jumping step which is fun to do. Its movement is like a cat pouncing on a mouse.

You travel sideways through the air in a light, springing movement, often doing several in succession.

You can do them to your right or to your left. These pictures show you how to do them to your left.

Arms in third and head looking over curved arm.

From a *demi-plié* in fifth, right foot in front, jump to the left so the toes of the left leg are level with the knees of the right leg.

Now raise your right leg to meet the left leg in the *retiré* position and turn your head further round to the left.

This is called the *retiré* position.

Finally land in a *demi-plié* in fifth position with your right foot in front. You will be standing to the left of your starting position.

The Dance of the Cats

Pas de chat is used in the Dance of the Cats, in Act 3 of *The Sleeping Beauty*. It was created by the great choreographer of Classical ballets, Marius Petipa. He translated a cat's natural movements into classical ballet steps.

Assemblés

In an *assemblé* you jump with your feet apart and bring them together (assemble them) before you land.

It is a versatile step because it can be done to the front, back or side and can be a small or very large jump.

On the right you can find out how to do one of the simpler *assemblé* jumping steps.

Arms in fifth *en bas*.

Place your feet in fifth, with your right leg in front and do a *demi-plié*. Then slide your left foot to second and raise it.

As your left foot reaches second, spring off your right foot, into the air. Open your arms out to second.

Incline your head to your left.

Left leg in front.

Bring both feet together to meet in the air and land in a *demi-plié* in fifth position. Bring your arms back to fifth *en bas*.

Elevation

One of the aims of a classical ballet dancer is to jump lightly and travel gracefully. The ability to jump high and with ease is known as having good elevation. Usually men are expected to jump higher than women and to turn more times.

35

A simple dance

Here is a simple dance which you can practise at home. Before you try it, make sure you have plenty of room and are warmed up. The dance is mostly made up of steps described on the last few pages. The names of the steps are shown on the piece of paper on the far right. It ends with a new turning step called a *soutenu*.

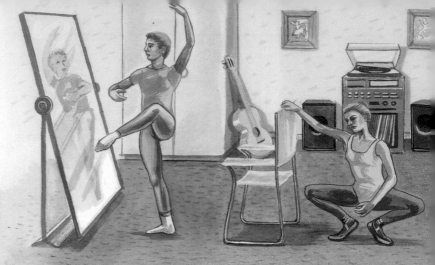

Glissade derrière

Arms in
fifth
en bas.

Incline
your head
to your left.

As your arms reach *demi-seconde*, raise your left foot about 7cm (3in) and point it.

Place your feet in fifth position with your right foot in front and do a *demi-plié*.

Slide your left foot to second position and open your arms through first into *demi-seconde*.

Then spring to the left. As you land, stretch your right foot off the ground, by about 7cm (3in).

Two *changements*

 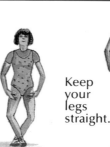  

Keep
your
legs
straight.

Straighten your legs and head, so you are looking directly to the front. Then do a *demi-plié*.

Now spring with straight legs into the air and swap the positions of your legs before landing.

Land in a *demi-plié* in fifth, right foot in front. Then spring into the air for the second *changement*.

Change your legs before landing, so you land with your left leg in front. Then straighten your legs.

Soutenu

   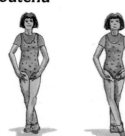   

Open your
arms out
to second.

Lower your arms to fifth *en bas*. Make a small circle with the right leg, bringing it round your left leg.

This carries you into a turn to your left. Turn on the ball of your foot. Bring your feet to fifth position.

Continue the turn on tiptoe, moving your arms through fifth *en avant* up to fifth *en haut*.

End with your left foot in front, so you are ready to repeat the *enchainement*, this time to the right.

In ballet, steps like the ones in this simple dance are joined together like words to make a sentence. These sentences are called *enchaînements*, which means links. The steps are like the links in a chain.

A solo of variation in a ballet is made up of several *enchaînements* put together.

Glissade derrière (to the left)
Assemblé dessus (to the left)
Two changements (on the spot)
Two pas de chats (to the right)
Soutenu (on the spot)

Assemblé dessus

Bring arms to fifth *en bas*.

Slide your right foot back to a *demi-plié* in fifth. Lower your arms through first, to fifth *en bas*.

Slide your left foot to second, about 7cm (3in) off the ground. Open your arms to *demi-seconde*.

Just as your foot reaches second, spring in the air off your right foot. Lean your head to the left.

Bring both legs together in the air to meet and land gently in a *demi-plié*, with your left foot in front.

Two *pas de chats*

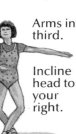

Arms in third.

Incline head to your right.

This is the *retiré* position.

From a *demi-plié*, jump to the right and bring the toes of your right leg to meet your left knee.

Raise your left leg to meet the toes of your right leg. Then land in a *demi-plié*, with the left leg in front.

Again, jump to the right, bringing the toes of your right leg to meet your left knee.

Raise your left leg to the *retiré* position. Land in a *demi-plié*, with your left leg in front.

Changing the *Enchaînement*

When you have practised the *enchaînement* a few times, try doing it at different speeds, as *petit* and *grand allegro*.

When this *enchaînement* is done quickly it has quite a different feel to it than when done slowly.

Once you have mastered the *enchaînement*, try to work out how to "beat" the *assemblé* and the *changements*. Beats are small, fast opening and closing movements of your legs, lightly beating your calves together in the air.

Steps for two

When a boy and girl dance together it is called *pas-de-deux* (steps for two). The *pas-de-deux* sections are the centre-pieces of most ballets. They usually express intense emotion such as love, grief or joy.

It takes years of practice and complete confidence in your partner to dance *pas-de-deux* well. Margot Fonteyn and Rudolf Nureyev were famous partners, as are Antoinette Sibley and Anthony Dowell.

Training for *pas-de-deux*

Pas-de-deux is usually taught in full-time ballet schools after the dancers have received a thorough training in all other aspects of ballet technique. The qualities required of the male and female dancer are different but equally demanding.

A boy must have the strength and control to lift the girl without overbalancing or dropping her.

Early training for boys includes weight-lifting to increase their strength. This is carefully regulated so that they do not develop bulky muscles which would spoil their streamlined appearance and slow them down.

Girls must be light but they also need strength, particularly in their wrists for hand grips. They also need strong feet and legs for dancing *en pointe* (see opposite).

Most of a girl's early training for *pas-de-deux* involves practice to develop her balance. The boy practices weight bearing exercises with the girl before moving on to the more difficult lifts and turns.

Developments in *pas-de-deux*

◄ This *pas-de-deux* from the Romantic era has a soft, dreamy look about it.

This *pas-de-deux* from ► a Classical ballet has more vitality than that of the Romantic ballet and the girl's leg is raised higher.

Modern ballets ► often bring partners into unexpected positions, like this one.

In the Romantic ballets of the mid-19th century, the ballerina was much more important than the male dancer. The men became known as *porteurs* (porters) because their job in a *pas-de-deux* was to carry the ballerina around.

Lifts were simple and the woman was mostly supported from behind.

In Classical ballets, *pas-de-deux* were made more dramatic and exciting.

Nowadays, due to Russian influence, lifts are more difficult and daring. Both partners take equal roles, though the male is always the support.

In many Modern ballets *pas-de-deux* is athletic and even gymnastic.

Dancing en pointe

Dancing *en pointe* means dancing on the tips of your toes.

The first ballerina to do this was Marie Taglioni, in the Romantic ballet *La Sylphide* (1832). She was trying to create the impression of a fairy-like creature, defying gravity.

It is important that you do not try to go *en pointe* until your ankles and feet are strong enough. Most girls are around 12 years old before they have enough strength to go *en pointe*. Do not try it without the guidance of a qualified teacher.

Men very rarely dance *en pointe*. One example, though, occurs in Frederick Ashton's ballet, *The Dream*. In this ballet, the character Bottom is magically turned into a donkey and dances *en pointe* to create the impression of an animal's hooves.

Pointe shoes

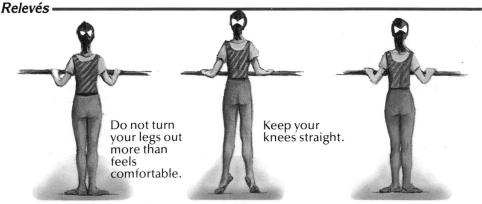

The ribbons help support the ankles.

Dancers sew on the ribbon themselves in the best place for their foot.

For dancing *en pointe* you need special satin slippers with stiffened toes. The toe part is made by "blocking" it with glue and baking it in an oven to harden and strengthen it.

Pointe shoes are very expensive because they are made by hand. The way they are made is kept secret by craftsmen who each have their own method.

A company dancer may get through up to ten pairs of *pointe* shoes a month. They do not wear out, but the glue softens and the shoes lose their support.

During a performance a ballerina may change shoes between scenes, using a softer pair for the *pas-de-deux* and harder pairs for *pirouettes* and hops *en pointe*.

Pointe technique

When dancing *en pointe*, lift your weight off your feet by keeping your knees straight and pulling up out of your hips. Your weight should be centred through your leg and foot.

The exercises below, called *relevés*, strengthen your feet, ankles and legs in preparation for *pointe* work.

Relevés

Do not turn your legs out more than feels comfortable.

Keep your knees straight.

Face the *barre*, resting both hands on it lightly. Turn your feet and legs out from the hips and pull your knees up tight.

Rise on to the balls of your feet and press them into the floor, making sure you can feel all your toes on the floor.

Then very slowly lower your heels back to the floor. Keep your legs straight and pull your knees tightly as you do so.

Problems with going en pointe

Going *en pointe* puts a lot of pressure on your toes and it does hurt. When you first start you may get blisters or your toes may bleed.

Experienced dancers only usually notice discomfort when they are standing still. However, many ballerinas develop bunions because the pressure forces the joint of their big toe out of line.

Famous choreographers

On these two pages you can find out about some famous choreographers and what influenced their work. The stories of some of the ballets they created are told on pages 42-43.

Choreographers fall into four main categories: Romantic, Classical, those of Diaghilev's company and Modern. Diaghilev's ideas paved the way for Modern ballet.

Romantic choreographers

Romanticism was a mood which influenced music, art and literature during the first half of the 19th century. People escaped from the depressing greyness of the Industrial Revolution into an imaginary world of faraway castles, spirits and the supernatural. The ballets created during this period reflect this interest in the supernatural.

Great importance was placed on the ballerina, whose gentle and passive image was idolized by a male-dominated, industrial society.

Scene from *La Sylphide.*

Although Paris was the centre of the ballet world at that time, two of the most famous choreographers were an Italian, Filippo Taglioni and a Danish ballet master, Bournonville, who later directed the Royal Danish Ballet.

While in Paris, Taglioni created *La Sylphide* in 1832 for his daughter, Marie, who typified the fairy-like, Romantic ballerina. In 1836, Bournonville created his own version of *La Sylphide* for a favourite pupil, Lucile Grahn.

Marie Taglioni

Jules Perrot

Jules Perrot was an important Romantic dancer and choreographer. He created the ballet *Giselle.*

Classical choreographers

Starting with Perrot in 1840, a succession of French choreographers went to Russia to work with the Imperial Russian Ballet in St Petersburg (now Leningrad). The company was financed by the Tsar and employed a composer to write music.

The extravagance of the Imperial Court is reflected in the Classical ballets created at this time. Their principle function was to display brilliant technique. The women dancers were therefore statuesque, rather than light and ethereal.

Perrot's first successor was St Leon who created *Coppélia,* to the music of Delibes. Then came the most famous Classical choreographer, Marius Petipa. With his colleague, Lev Ivanov and the composer Tchaikovsky, he created the great Classical ballets, *The Sleeping Beauty* (1890), *The Nutcracker* (1892) and *Swan Lake* (1895).

Petipa

Ivanov

Tchaikovsky

A costume for *The Nutcracker.*

The Classical ballets are made up of three or four acts and contain complex arrangements for the *corps de ballet* and *pas de deux*. A *pas de deux* is often followed by a male solo and then a female solo, created purely to show off the dancers' skill and technique.

Diaghilev choreographers

Petipa's successor at the Russian Ballet was Mikhail Fokine. He broke away from the formal structures of the earlier ballets. He made one-act ballets and used male dancers equally with ballerinas. In 1905 he created a solo, *The Dying Swan*, for Anna Pavlova.

Anna Pavlova

Fokine collaborated with a man called Diaghilev, whose brilliance lay in directing and co-ordinating the genius of others, whether they were dancers, choreographers, composers or designers. Between 1909 and 1929 Diaghilev's Russian Ballet, also known as the Ballet Russe, toured Europe revitalizing ballet and attracting new talent wherever it went.

Diaghilev had tremendous artistic vision, giving equal weight to dance, music and design. For example, under Diaghilev's guidance, Fokine joined forces with the composer Stravinsky and the designer Benois, to produce the ballet *Petrushka* in 1911.

Costume for Petrushka.

The changes of the 1910s, 20s and 30s, such as greater freedom for women, the jazz age, the First World War and the increased opportunity for sport and travel, are all reflected in Diaghilev's progressive ballets. The revolutionary impact of these changes can be seen in a ballet such as *L'Après-midi d'un Faune*, created by one of Diaghilev's protegés, Nijinsky. His ballet rejected every rule of turn-out and classical presentation of the body. This new style echoed the growing movement of contemporary dance.

Modern choreographers

After Diaghilev died in 1929, the members of his company spread their talents throughout Europe, Russia and America. George Balanchine, one of Diaghilev's stars, went to the USA to form the New York City Ballet. There he created a unique American classical ballet style with works such as *The Prodigal Son, Stars and Stripes* and *Serenade*.

Serge Lifar, Diaghilev's last male star, became director of the Paris Opéra Company, where he created such ballets as *Noir et Blanc*. Leonid Massine, also of the Ballet Russe, created roles in films such as *Red Shoes* which he did with Robert Helpmann.

In Britain, Marie Rambert started her own company, Ballet Rambert and Ninette de Valois founded the Sadler's Wells Theatre Ballet. This later became two companies, the Royal Ballet and Sadler's Wells Royal Ballet. De Valois encouraged young choreographers such as Kenneth MacMillan and John Cranko, who revitalized the Stuttgart Ballet in the 60s. She created her own works, too, such as *The Rake's Progress*.

Scene from *La Fille Mal Gardée*.

Two later directors of the Royal Ballet have created many works. Sir Frederick Ashton has made short ballets and full length works in the tradition of Petipa, for example, *La Fille Mal Gardée* and *Romeo and Juliet* for the Royal Danish Ballet. Kenneth MacMillan's dramatic works include *Mayerling* and *Manon*. He has prepared many of his ballets for staging by the American Ballet Theater.

Ballet today

Classical ballet continues to develop under choreographers such as David Bintley, who has created short and full length ballets, such as *Snow Queen*, for the Royal Ballet.

The Danish ballet star, Peter Schaufuss, now directs the London Festival Ballet, staging new works and directing revivals of older ballets.

In America, Glen Tetley continues to make exciting ballets, often combining classical ballet and modern dance. Another inspiring choreographer is Jiri Kylian of the Netherland's Dance Theatre. The National Ballet of Canada staged his ballet, *Transfigured Night*, in 1986. Constantin Patsalas, the National Ballet of Canada's own choreographer, has created almost 30 works, including the famous *Piano Concerto*.

Stories of ballets

Here is a selection of stories from Romantic, Classical and Modern ballets. There are also some ballets from the Diaghilev era. These came between Classical and Modern ballets.

Romantic ballets

La Sylphide

Choreography: Taglioni
Music: Scheitzhoeffner

James dreams of a fairy creature, the Sylphide, on the eve of his wedding to Effie. The Sylphide teasingly declares her love for him and snatches away Effie's ring. On the advice of a witch, James wraps the Sylphide in a scarf, to prevent her flying away. Her wings fall off and she dies. James is heartbroken, since by now his best friend has married Effie.

Giselle

Choreography: Coralli/Perrot
Music: Adam

Giselle loves Loys, whom she thinks is a poor country dweller, like herself. Loys is Count Albrecht. Giselle's fiancé, Hilarion, betrays Albrecht's secret. Giselle kills herself and joins the Wilis (spirits of girls who have died before their wedding night and seek revenge on men). They have killed Hilarion but Albrecht is saved from the same fate by Giselle's devotion.

Classical ballets

Coppélia

Choreography: St Leon and others.
Music: Delibes

Dr Coppélius makes a doll, Coppélia. Swanhilda's fiancé, Franz, falls in love with Coppélia and Dr Coppélius tries to bring her to life with a spell. Swanhilda pretends to be Coppélia, but Franz recognizes her. They are reunited.

The Nutcracker

The Nutcracker

Choreography: Ivanov
Music: Tchaikovsky

Clara is given a Nutcracker for Christmas. At night all her gifts come to life. Clara rescues the Nutcracker from a fight between toy soldiers and some mice. He takes her to the Kingdom of Sweets, where fairytale characters entertain her.

The Sleeping Beauty

Choreography: Petipa
Music: Tchaikovsky

In revenge for not being invited to Princess Aurora's christening, the wicked fairy Carabosse says Aurora will prick her finger and die on her 16th birthday. The Lilac Fairy lessens the spell by promising Aurora will fall asleep for 100 years and be woken by a prince's kiss. This happens and the Prince and Princess marry.

Swan Lake

Choreography: Petipa/Ivanov
Music: Tchaikovsky

While hunting, Prince Siegfried sees a swan, who changes into a young woman. She is Odette who has been turned into a swan by a wicked magician, Von Rothbart. The spell will only be broken if a man falls in love with her.

Von Rothbart presents his daughter, Odile, in the guise of Odette. Siegfried promises to love Odile and then realizes his mistake when a vision of Odette appears. Rothbart raises a storm on the lake and Odette kills herself. Siegfried follows her into the lake and the spell is broken.

Diaghilev ballets

The Dying Swan

Choreography: Fokine
Music: Saint-Saens

The Dying Swan is a solo dance, portraying the fluttering of a swan as it nears death. It was created for Anna Pavlova.

Firebird

Choreography: Fokine
Music: Stravinsky

Prince Ivan captures a Firebird. When he releases her, she gives him a magic feather to protect him. He later rescues a group of princesses, captured by the evil Kostchei and his monsters. Ivan marries the chief princess, Tsarevna.

Petrushka

Choreography: Fokine
Music: Stravinksy

A showman proves to his audience that his puppets (a Moor, a ballerina and Petrushka) come to life when he plays his flute. The crowd is horrified when Petrushka is killed in a fight with the Moor over the ballerina. The showman reminds them Petrushka is only a puppet. However, Petrushka's ghost rises to mock him.

Modern ballets

Le Spectre de la Rose

Choreography: Fokine
Music: Weber

A girl kisses the rose she has been wearing before dropping asleep. It falls to the floor and its spirit appears through the window. In the morning she remembers her dream but the rose has wilted.

Les Sylphides

The Sylphes

Choreography: Fokine
Music: Chopin (arr. Stravinsky)

This ballet has no real story. A young man, possibly a poet, dances with the spirits of young women (Sylphes). The ballet ends with the Sylphes encircling the poet, who is reluctant to leave.

L'Après-midi d'un Faune

Choreography: Nijinsky
Music: Debussy

A lonely faun is lying by a pool. He scares away all but one of a group of nymphs. She escapes when he becomes too friendly, but later creeps back to rescue a scarf she has dropped. She finds the faun comforting himself with the scarf, so she leaves him with his trophy.

The Rite of Spring

Choreography: Nijinsky
Music: Stravinsky

This ballet enacts a primitive ritual, celebrating the arrival of Spring. A girl is chosen as a human sacrifice by the elders. She has to dance till she falls dead from exhaustion.

Stars and Stripes

Choreography: Balanchine
Music: Sousa

Stars and Stripes conveys the spirit of the USA, with prancing drum majorettes and military drill. There are three groups of performers, dressed in patriotic costumes.

The Prodigal Son

Choreography: Balanchine
Music: Prokofiev

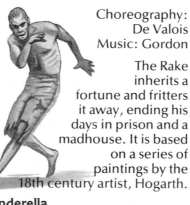

The Prodigal Son is based on a biblical parable. A son leaves home and joins a crowd of revellers, who rob him of everything. He drags himself home, fearing his father will not forgive him but he is welcomed.

The Rake's Progress

Choreography: De Valois
Music: Gordon

The Rake inherits a fortune and fritters it away, ending his days in prison and a madhouse. It is based on a series of paintings by the 18th century artist, Hogarth.

Cinderella

Choreography: Ashton and others
Music: Prokofiev

Cinderella is left at home while her stepsisters go to a Ball. A Fairy Godmother transforms Cinderella's rags into a ballgown and diamond slippers but warns her they will return to rags at midnight. At the Ball, the Prince falls in love with her. She runs away at midnight dropping a slipper. The Prince says he will marry whom the slipper fits. After a long search he finds Cinderella.

The Dream

Choreography: Ashton
Music: Mendelssohn

This is a one-act ballet of Shakespeare's play *A Midsummer Night's Dream*. It centres round an argument between Titania and Oberon over a mysterious Indian Boy, and the loves of Helena, Hermia, Demetrius and Lysander.

La Fille Mal Gardée

Farmyard scene from *La Fille Mal Gardée*.

Choreography: Ashton
Music: Hérold (arr. Lanchbery)

Lise loves Colas, a young farmer. Her mother, widow Simone, wants her to marry Alain, the clumsy son of a rich farmer. After many amusing adventures, widow Simone lets Lise marry Colas.

Romeo and Juliet

Choreography: Ashton, Macmillan and others
Music: Prokofiev

This ballet is based on a Shakespeare play. Romeo and Juliet come from feuding families. They fall in love and are secretly married, though Juliet is engaged to Paris. Romeo is banished after a fight. Juliet takes a sleeping potion to make her appear dead, so she will not have to marry Paris. Romeo thinks she is "dead" and kills himself. Juliet awakes, finds Romeo dead and kills herself.

Manon

Choreography: MacMillan
Music: Massenet

The ballet is based on an 18th century French novel about a young girl, Manon Lescaut, who is led astray by Parisian society. Chevalier des Grieux falls in love with her but Manon is deported to the swamps of Louisiana.

Famous dancers

These two pages tell you about some famous ballet dancers, past and present.

Barishnikov, Mikhail (born 1948)

Mikhail Barishnikov was born in Russia and studied at the Kirov Ballet School. He later left Russia to dance in the West.

He has danced with both the Royal Ballet, where he made his début in 1975 and the American Ballet Theater, where he became Director in 1980. He has danced both modern and classical works and appeared in several ballet films, including *The Turning Point* (1978) and *White Nights* (1986).

Bujones, Fernando (born 1955)

Fernando Bujones was born in Miami. He studied ballet in Cuba (his parents were Cuban), Miami and New York, and became a principal with the American Ballet Theater. He has made guest appearances all over the world, dancing a variety of roles, including ones created especially for him. In 1985 he danced at the White House for the American President and also made his début with the Royal Ballet.

Collier, Lesley (born 1947)

Lesley Collier was born in England and began dancing at the age of two. She went to the Royal Ballet School and joined the Company in 1965. She has danced roles in all the great classical ballets, including Juliet in Kenneth MacMillan's *Romeo and Juliet* (1973) and Lise in *La Fille Mal Gardée* (1970).

Sir Frederick Ashton created *Rhapsody* for Collier and Barishnikov for the English Queen Mother's 80th birthday in 1980.

Dolin, Anton (1904-1983)

Diaghilev spotted the English dancer, Anton Dolin (Patrick Kay) at the age of 19. This resulted in Dolin appearing in *The Sleeping Beauty* for the Ballet Russe.

In 1928 he began a famous partnership with Alicia Markova. They formed the Markova-Dolin Ballet Company in 1935. Later in life he turned increasingly to choreography and directing.

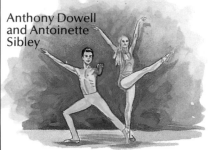

Anthony Dowell and Antoinette Sibley

Dowell, Anthony (born 1943)

London-born Anthony Dowell trained at the Royal Ballet School and joined the Company in 1962.

He danced Oberon in the first production of *The Dream* in 1964. This began his partnership with Antoinette Sibley.

He is especially good at bringing to life heroes such as Albrecht (*Giselle*), Prince Siegfried (*Swan Lake*) and Prince Florimund (*The Sleeping Beauty*).

He spent a year dancing with the American Ballet Theater in 1978 and became Director of the Royal Ballet in September 1986.

Eagling, Wayne (born 1950)

Wayne Eagling was born in Canada. He went to the Royal Ballet School in London and joined the Company in 1969.

In 1973, he danced Romeo for the first time with Lesley Collier. He has since danced leading roles in many major ballets.

In 1986 he created a new ballet, *Frankenstein*, with music by Vangelis and costumes by Emanuel.

Fonteyn, Margot (1919-1991)

Margot Fonteyn studied at the Sadler's Wells Ballet School in London where she was singled out as a soloist at the age of 16.

She is well known for two long and famous partnerships. The first was with Michael Somes and the second was with Rudolf Nureyev after his defection from Russia in 1962. By then Sir Frederick Ashton had created many roles for her. Her partnership with Nureyev inspired still more.

Makarova, Natalia (born 1940)

Natalia Makarova is Russian. She trained at the Leningrad Ballet School and joined the Kirov Ballet in 1959. In 1970 she left the company while the Kirov were appearing in London and joined the American Ballet Theater.

There is a fragile quality to her dancing, which makes her excel in roles such as Giselle.

She appeared in the musical *On Your Toes* and is continuing her career in musical theatre.

Alicia Markova

Markova, Alicia (born 1910)

Alicia Markova joined Diaghilev's Ballet Russe at the age of 14 after Anton Dolin persuaded Diaghilev to watch her dance. Markova was Sadler's Wells' first prima ballerina. She formed the Markova-Dolin Company with Anton Dolin in 1935.

Mitchell, Arthur (born 1934)

Arthur Mitchell went to Balanchine's School of American Ballet. This was unusual as he is black and at that time there were no black classical ballet dancers. He later joined the New York City Ballet.

In 1969 he formed an all black company, the Dance Theater of Harlem, in response to the murder of the black civil rights leader Martin Luther King. His company is now internationally famous and performs all over the world.

Nijinsky, Vaslav (1890-1950)

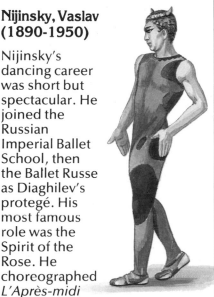

Nijinsky's dancing career was short but spectacular. He joined the Russian Imperial Ballet School, then the Ballet Russe as Diaghilev's protégé. His most famous role was the Spirit of the Rose. He choreographed *L'Après-midi d'un Faune* (1912), followed by *The Rite of Spring* in 1913.

Nureyev, Rudolf (1938-1993)

The Russian dancer Rudolf Nureyev began his training at the late age of 17.

While in Paris in 1961, he left the Kirov Ballet to dance in the West. The following year he made a spectacular début with the Royal Ballet in *Giselle*. This was the beginning of a legendary partnership with Margot Fonteyn, which inspired many new ballets.

Nureyev is now Director of the Paris Opéra Ballet and still makes guest appearances with companies all over the world.

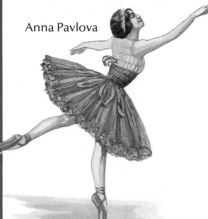

Anna Pavlova

Pavlova, Anna (1882-1931)

Anna Pavlova joined the Imperial Ballet School in St Petersburg (Leningrad) and danced all the principal roles in Petipa's ballets at the Maryinsky Theatre.

She later danced with the Ballet Russe and formed her own company.

She is most remembered for her solo, *The Dying Swan*.

Seymour, Lynn (born 1939)

Canadian-born Lynn Seymour trained at the Royal Ballet School in London. She joined the Royal Ballet Company in 1957, left to dance with the Deutsche Opera in 1966 and returned to the Royal Ballet in 1970.

Her dramatic dancing inspired MacMillan to create many roles for her, including Juliet.

She was guest artist with many companies and, before retiring, directed the Munich Ballet.

Schaufuss, Peter (born 1949)

Peter Schaufuss was born in Denmark, the son of Danish ballet stars. Since leaving the Danish Ballet School he has danced with the National Ballet of Canada, the London Festival Ballet, the Kirov and Bolshoi Ballets, the New York City Ballet and others.

He is now an established artist, producer and choreographer with companies all over the world. In 1994 he became Director of the Royal Danish Ballet.

Sibley, Antoinette (born 1939)

Antoinette Sibley is a British dancer. She trained at the Royal Ballet School and is a member of the Royal Ballet Company.

She is particularly famous for her interpretation of roles, especially Titania in *The Dream*, Dora Penny in *Enigma Variations* and the title role in Kenneth MacMillan's *Manon*.

Her famous partnership with Anthony Dowell began in 1964.

She played Sevilla in the film *The Turning Point*.

Wayne Sleep is very good in comic roles.

Sleep, Wayne (born 1948)

Wayne Sleep trained at the Royal Ballet School and joined the Company in 1966. His lack of height is an asset in certain roles such as Puck in *The Dream*. He was also one of the Two Bad Mice in the film *The Tales of Beatrix Potter*.

Sleep left classical ballet to pursue a career in musical theatre. He formed his own company, Dash, and appeared in a successful TV series, *The Hot Shoe Show* which he took on tour.

Taglioni, Marie (1804-1884)

Marie Taglioni was the first dancer to break away from tradition by dancing *en pointe*. She was trained mainly by her father, Filippo Taglioni. She created the title role in *La Sylphide*, the ballet which marked the birth of Romantic ballet.

Ballet words

A la quatrième derrière. In fourth position behind. (One of the eight **positions of the body** in **classical** ballet.)

A la quatrième devant. In fourth position in front. (One of the eight **positions of the body** in **classical** ballet.)

A la seconde. In second position. (One of the eight **positions of the body** in **classical** ballet.)

Adage. Slow, sustained movements.

Administrative director. The person responsible for a company's major policy decisions.

Alignment. The lining up of parts of your body to make a balanced and graceful outline.

Allegro. An Italian musical term meaning quick. In ballet, *allegro* steps are fast steps.

Arabesque. A position in which you balance on one leg with the other stretched out behind you.

Artistic director. The person in a company who decides which ballets will be performed and who will dance each role.

Assemblé. A travelling step in which you jump with feet apart and bring them together before landing.

Assessment. A check on a ballet student's progress.

Attitude. A position in which you stand on one leg and lift and curve the other leg round behind you.

Backcloth. A large cloth hanging down at the back of the stage on which scenery is painted.

Ballerina. A female dancer of **principal** or **soloist** status.

Ballet master or mistress. The person who rehearses ballets and supervises the *corps de ballet.*

Barre. A wooden hand rail that runs round the walls of a ballet **studio.** It is used to aid balance while doing exercises.

Barrel turn. A type of leap in which the dancer travels in a large circle.

Battement frappé. An exercise in which you cross your heel alternately in front and behind the ankle of your supporting leg, pointing your leg to the side between each position.

Battement glissé. An exercise in which you slide your foot along the ground and lift it.

Battement tendu. An exercise in which you stretch your foot along the floor to the front, side, back and side again (*en croix*).

Beating. Rapid, opening and closing movements of stretched legs during a jump.

Benesh notation. A system of dance **notation.** It was developed by Rudolf and Joan Benesh.

Bourées. A series of tiny steps which give the impression of gliding along the floor.

Call sheet. A rehearsal timetable for dancers in a company.

Cecchetti technique. One of the techniques of **classical** ballet.

Centre practice. Exercise done in the middle of the **studio** without the support of the *barre.*

Changement. A jump in which you take off with one leg in front and land with the other leg in front.

Changement battu. A *changement* in which you **beat** your legs before landing.

Choreographer. Someone who creates, or choreographs, ballets by putting steps to music.

Choreologist. Someone who writes dance steps down using **notation**.

Classical. A term used to describe ballet technique. Also used to describe ballets of the latter half of the 19th century which display classical ballet in its purest form.

Contemporary dance. A modern style of dance, less rigid in structure than **classical** ballet.

Corps de ballet. A large group of dancers in a ballet who perform the same steps.

Coryphée. A leader of the *corps de ballet* or a dance on the way to becoming a **soloist.**

Coupe jeté en tournant. See **Barrel turn.**

Croisé devant. Crossed in front. (One of the eight **positions of the body** in **classical** ballet.)

Croisée derrière. Crossed behind. (One of the eight **positions of the body** in **classical** ballet.)

Cross-over. A type of cardigan worn in class which crosses over at the front and ties at the back.

Curtain up. The start of a performance when the stage curtains rise.

Demi-plié. A half knee-bend.

Demi-pointe. Half point i.e. standing on the balls of your feet.

Demi-seconde. An arm position half way between first and second positions.

Développé. An exercise in which you slowly raise and unfold your leg.

Education officer. The person in a company who organizes contacts with schools and the community.

Effacé. Turned away. (One of the eight **positions of the body** in **classical** ballet.)

Elancer. To dart. One of the seven **movements of dance**.

Elevation. The ability to jump high, with ease.

En avant. Above. (One of the eight **positions of the body** in **classical** ballet.)

En bas. Below. A term used to describe the arms when held low.

En croix. In the shape of a cross. It describes exercises done to the front, side, back and side again.

En dedans. To the inside. It describes a turn towards the supporting leg.

En dehors. To the outside. It describes a turn away from the supporting leg.

En haut. High. A term used to describe the arms when held above the head.

En pointe. Standing or dancing on the tips of your toes.

En relevé. On the balls of your feet.

Enchaînement. A series of steps linked together to make a dance sequence.

Ensemble. A group formation of dancers in some **Modern** ballets.

Entrechat. A jump in which you take off with one foot in front, change your feet over and then change them back before landing.

Epaulé. Shouldered. (One of the eight **positions of the body** in **classical** ballet.)

First night. The opening performance of a ballet.

Fish dive. A step in which the man catches the woman as she swoops towards the ground in a fish-like movement.

Fish step. See *temps de poisson*.

Glissade. A travelling step in which you glide your foot along the ground and transfer your weight on to it.

Glisser. To glide. One of the seven **movements of dance**.

Graduation performance. A performance at the end of ballet students' training at which the most promising dancers are chosen to join the company.

Grand allegro. Large jumping and travelling steps.

Grand battement. An exercise in which you point your foot and raise it.

Grand jeté. A leap through the air with legs outstretched.

Grand plié. A full knee-bend.

Labanotation. A system of dance **notation**. It was devised by Rudolf von Laban.

Mime. A set of gestures each with a particular meaning which help to tell a story.

Modern. A term used to describe ballets created during the latter half of this century.

Movements of dance. Seven types of dance movement based on natural movements of the body.

Notation. Systems of signs used to record dance steps on paper.

Pas de bourrées. A travelling step done to a *bourrée*, or type of dance music.

Pas de chat. Step of a cat. A travelling step.

Pas-de-deux. Steps where a boy and girl partner each other.

Petit allegro. Small jumping and turning steps.

Petit battement sur le coup de pied. An exercise in which you alternately cross your heel in front and behind the ankle of your supporting leg.

Physiotherapist. A person trained to treat dancers' injuries.

Pigs' ears. The name given to untidy ends of ballet shoe ribbons that stick out after being tied.

Pirouette. A turning step, meaning a whirl.

Pit. Where the orchestra sit, below the front of the stage.

Placing. The position of one part of your body in relation to another.

Plié. A knee-bend.

Plier. To bend. One of the seven **movements of dance**.

Pointe shoes. Block-toed ballet shoes used for dancing **en pointe**.

Port de bras. Set movements of the arms from one position to another.

Positions of the body. Eight different ways of standing and holding your arms which show off the line of your body when doing **centre practice**.

Positions of the feet. Five different positions in which your weight is evenly distributed over your feet whatever position your body is in.

Premier danseur. A title which can be given to a **principal** male dancer.

Press officer. The person in a company who maintains contact with the Press, informing them of a company's future performances.

Principal. A dancer who performs a leading role in a ballet.

Relever. To rise. One of the seven **movements of dance**.

Relevé. An exercise in which you rise up on the balls of your feet.

Répétiteur. A person who rehearses ballets with the dancers.

Rig. The arrangement of stage lights.

Romantic. A term used to describe the style of ballet created during the Romantic era in the first half of the 19th century.

Rondes de jambes à terre. An exercise in which you mark out a semi-circle on the ground with your pointed foot.

Rosin. A yellow crystal which breaks down into a white powder. Dancers rub the soles of their shoes in it to stop them slipping.

Set. The scenery and props on the stage.

Soloist. A dancer who dances alone, or solo, in a ballet.

Soutenu. A turning step.

Spotting. A technique used by dancers to stop them becoming giddy when turning fast.

Stage manager. The person who co-ordinates the lighting, scene changes, dancers and so on during a performance of a ballet.

Stave. Five parallel lines on which music or dance **notation** can be written.

Studio. A room where ballet classes are held.

Technical director. The person in charge of the lighting, special effects and so on in a ballet.

Temps de poisson. A jump in which the dancer bends his body like a fish.

Theatre craft. The art of performing to an audience.

Tourner. To turn. One of the seven **movements of dance**.

Turn-out. The technique belonging to **classical** ballet of turning the legs out to the side from the hip sockets.

Tutu. A ballet costume with a fitted bodice and a short, sticking out skirt. Characteristic of **Classical** ballet.

Wardrobe. The costume department of a ballet company.

Warm-up. Simple exercises at the start of a class which prepare the muscles for more demanding movements.

Index

adage steps, 31, 33, 46
Adam, 42
alignment, 9, 46
allegro, 9, 30, 33, 34-35, 46, 47
American Ballet Theater, 41, 44
Après-midi d'un Faune, L', 41, 43, 45
arabesque, 7, 11, 30, 31, 46
Ashton, Sir Frederick, 41, 43, 44
assemblé, 35, 37, 46
assessment, 25, 46
attitude, 31, 33, 46
audition, 24
Australian Ballet, 25
Balanchine, George, 11, 25, 41, 43, 45
ballet,
  class, 3, 4, 8, 9, 24-25
  companies, 21, 22, 23
  master/mistress, 15, 23, 46
  school, 22, 24
  shoes, 4, 5, 17, 39
  steps, 3, 6, 7, 30-35
  teachers, 22, 23
Ballet Rambert, 41
Ballet Russe, 41, 44, 45
Barishnikov, Mikhail, 10, 44
barre, 8, 9, 46
  exercises, 26-27, 28-29, 39
barrel turn, 20, 46
battement frappé, 28-29, 46
battement glissé, 26-27, 46
battement tendu, 26-27, 46
beating, 34, 37, 46
Beauchamps, 3, 6
Benesh notation, 12-13, 46
Benois, 41
Bintley, David, 11, 41
Bolshoi Ballet, 25, 45
  Theatre, 21
Bournonville, Auguste, 25, 40
bourrées, 20, 46
British Ballet Organisation
  (B.B.O.), 7
Bujones, Fernando, 44
Camargo, Marie, 3
Canadian National Ballet, 25
  School, 25
Cecchetti,
  technique, 7, 26, 27, 46
centre practice/work, 8, 9, 30-31, 46
changement, 34, 36, 37, 46
  battu, 34, 46
choreographer, 3, 10-11, 15, 40-41, 42-43, 44, 45
choreography, 3, 10-11, 20, 23, 25, 42-43, 44-45
choreologist, 12, 13, 15, 46
choreology, 12-13, 25
Cinderella, 14, 19, 43
classical, 2, 3, 6, 7, 35, 41, 45, 46
  technique, 4, 5, 6, 7
Classical ballets, 2, 18, 35, 38, 40, 41, 42, 46, 47

Collier, Lesley, 44
Comic Ballet of the Queen, 3
Commedia del Arte, La, 3
contemporary dance, 12, 22, 23, 41, 46
Coppélia, 11, 40, 42
Coralli, 42
corps de ballet, 14-15, 20, 22, 40
coryphée, 12
costume, 3, 16, 17, 18-19
coup jeté en tournant (see barrel turn),
Cranko, John, 41
croix, en, 28, 46
Dance Theater of Harlem, 45
Danish Ballet School, 45
Debussy, 43
dedans, en, 28, 33, 46
dehors, en, 28, 33, 46
Delibes, 40, 42
Deutsche Oper, 45
développé, 28-29, 31, 46
Diaghilev, 20, 41, 42, 43, 44, 45
  ballets 41, 42-43
Dolin, Anton, 44
Dowell, Anthony 38, 44, 45
Dream, The, 38, 43, 44, 45
Dying Swan, The, 41, 42, 45
Eagling, Wayne, 11, 44
elevation, 35
enchaînement, 24, 36-37, 46
Enigma Variations, 18, 45
ensemble, 14, 47
Entrechat, 34
Fille Mal Gardée, La, 17, 21, 41, 44
Firebird, 42
fish,
  dive, 20, 47
  step (see *temps de poisson*),
Fokine, Mikhail, 41, 42, 43
Fonteyn, Margot, 38, 44
Frankenstein, 11, 44
Giselle, 2, 40, 42, 44, 45
glissade, 7, 32-33, 47
  derrière, 36, 37
Grahn, Lucile, 40
grand battement, 13, 28-29, 47
grand jeté, 11
Hérold, 43
Hot Shoe Show, The, 45
Imperial,
  Ballet School, 45
  Russian Ballet, 40
  Society Classical Ballet exam
    syllabus, 7
Ivanov, Lev, 40, 42
Kirov Ballet, 25, 44, 45
  School, 44
Kylian, Jiri, 41
Labanotation, 12, 47
Lanchbery, 43
Leningrad Ballet School, 44
Lifar, Serge, 41
London Festival Ballet, 41, 45
MacMillan, Kenneth, 10, 41, 43, 45

Makarova, Natalia, 44
make-up, 3, 17, 18-19
Manon, 41, 43, 45
Markova, Alicia, 44
Massenet, 43
Massine, Leonid, 41
Mayerling, 41
Mendelssohn, 43
Metropolitan Opéra House, 21
mime, 3, 20, 21, 47
Mitchell, Arthur, 45
Modern ballet, 2, 18, 20, 38, 41, 43
movements of dance, 6, 7, 47
Munich Ballet, 45
Mussorgsky, 11
National Ballet of Canada, 41, 45
Netherlands Dance Theatre, 41
New York City Ballet, 41, 45
  School, 22, 25
Nijinsky, Vaslav, 34, 41, 43, 45
Noir et Blanc, 41
notation, 3, 10, 12-13, 46, 47
Nureyev, Rudolf, 38, 44, 45
Nutcracker, The, 2, 21, 40, 42
On Your Toes, 44
Paris Opéra Ballet Company, 25, 41, 45
  School, 25
pas de bourrées, 32-33, 47
pas de chat, 7, 35, 37, 47
pas-de-deux, 38, 40, 47
Patsalas, Constantin, 41
Pavlova, Anna, 41, 45
Perrot, Jules, 40, 42
Petipa, Marius, 35, 40, 42, 45
petits battements sur le cou-de-pied, 28, 29, 47
Petrushka, 16, 41, 42
physiotherapist, 15, 47
Piano Concerto, 41
pirouette, 7, 32, 33, 39, 47
placing, 9, 47
plié, 9, 11, 26, 27
  demi-, 11, 26-27, 32, 33, 34, 35, 36, 37, 46
  grand, 13, 26-27, 47
pointe,
  demi-, 13, 46
  en, 5, 11, 20, 24, 38, 39, 45, 46
  shoes, 5, 17, 39, 47
ports de bras, 9, 30, 31, 47
positions
  of the arms, 26, 27
  of the body, 30, 46, 47
  of the feet, 3, 6, 26, 47
principal, 14-15, 46, 47
Prodigal Son, The, 18, 41, 43
Prokofiev, 43
Rake's Progress, The, 41, 43
Rambert, Marie, 41
Red Shoes, The, 41
relevés, 38, 39
répétiteur, 15, 47
retiré, 35
Rhapsody, 4

Rite of Spring, The, 43, 45
Romantic,
  ballet, 2, 18, 38, 39, 40, 41, 42, 45, 47
  Movement, 2, 40
Romeo and Juliet, 19, 41, 44
rondes de jambe à terre, 28-29, 47
Royal Academy of Dancing,
  Louis XIVs, 3, 6
  R.A.D., 7
Royal Ballet,
  Company, 41, 43, 45
  School, 22, 25, 44, 45
Royal Danish Ballet, 40, 41
  School, 25, 45
Royal Opera House, 21
Sadler's Wells Royal Ballet, 41, 44
Saint-Saens, 42
Schaufuss, Peter, 41, 45
Scheithoeffner, 42
Serenade, 41
Seymour, Lynn, 10, 45
Sibley, Antoinette, 38, 44, 45
Sleep, Wayne, 23, 34, 45
Sleeping Beauty, The, 2, 12, 14, 16, 35, 40, 42, 44
Snow Queen, 11, 41
solo, 14-14, 20, 37, 40, 41
Somes, Michael, 44
Sousa, 43
southenu, 36
Spectre de la Rose, Le, 18, 43
spotting, 32
St Leon, 40, 42
Stars and Stripes, 41, 43
Stravinsky, 11, 41, 42, 43
Stuttgart Ballet, 41
Swan Lake, 2, 11, 14, 40, 42, 44
Sydney Opera House, 21
Sylphide, La, 2, 39, 40, 42, 45
Sylphides, Les, 43
Taglioni,
  Filippo, 40, 42, 45
  Marie, 39, 40, 45
Tales of Beatrix Potter, The, 18, 45
Tchaikovsky, 40, 42
temps de poisson (fish step), 20, 47
Tetley, Glen, 41
Tovey, Branwell, 11
Transfigured Night, 41
turn-out, 6, 47
Turning point, The, 44, 45
tutu, 18, 19, 47
Twyla Tharp, 10
Valois, Ninette de, 41, 43
Vangelis, 11, 44
Violin Concerto, 11
wardrobe, 15, 16, 47
  master/mistress, 15
warm-up, 9, 47
Weber, 43
weight-lifting, 25, 38
White Nights, 44
wigs, 2, 17

Usborne Publishing would like to thank the following for use of photographs and other material for artistic reference.

Page 2, bottom left and centre © Anthony Crickmay; bottom right © Martha Swope.
Page 12 (top centre) and page 13, Benesh Movement Notation © Rudolf Benesh London 1955.
Page 18, bottom left © Roy Round; bottom right © Dominic Photography.
Illustration of a scene from the film "The Tales of Beatrix Potter" by kind permission of The Cannon Group UK Limited.
Page 19, bottom left © Leslie E. Spatt.
Page 20, top left © Camilla Jessel; top right © Martha Swope.
Page 38, top, bottom right and left © Leslie E. Spatt; centre © Camilla Jessel.
Page 43, top centre © Leslie E. Spatt; bottom centre © Dominic Photography.
Page 44, centre © Leslie E. Spatt.
Page 45, right © Roy Round.

First published in 1986 by Usborne Publishing Ltd, 83-85 Saffron Hill, London EC1N 8RT, England.